The Lav Legal Project Management

EDITED BY EDWARD BOWES

Head of events and books
Leah Darbyshire

Commissioning editor
Laura Slater

Editorial assistant
Edward Bowes

Published by ARK Group:

UK, Europe and Asia office
6–14 Underwood Street
London, N1 7JQ
United Kingdom
Tel: +44(0) 207 566 5792
publishing@ark-group.com

North America office
4408 N. Rockwood Drive, Suite 150
Peoria IL 61614
United States
Tel: +1 (309) 495 2853
publishingna@ark-group.com

www.ark-group.com

Layout by Susie Bell, www.f-12.co.uk

Printed by Canon (UK) Ltd, Cockshot Hill, Reigate, RH2 8BF, United Kingdom

ISBN: 978-1-78358-276-1

A catalogue record for this book is available from the British Library

ARK Group is a division of Wilmington plc. The company is registered in England & Wales with company number 2931372 GB
Registered office: 6-14 Underwood Street, London N1 7JQ. VAT Number: GB 899 3725 51.

Contents

Executive summary

Effectively implementing project management has become a key ambition for many firms across the world. The interest project management has garnered from the legal sector is not surprising; the range of benefits it offers are extensive and impactful; including reducing costs, enabling more efficient commodity work, and creating more accurate budgeting forecasts.

However, despite the general consensus on its value, adoption rates have been slow across the sector – only a handful of top firms have successfully implemented LPM into their practices, and are reaping the benefits. The slow adoption rates create a real opening for a competitive advantage through Legal Project Management, even at a basic starting level, as according to Jim Hassett even "glacial progress can produce new business when you are competing with firms that are making no progress at all".

The Lawyer's Guide to Legal Project Management is an invaluable asset for any firm looking to capitalize on the strategic gap in the market; whether it be though introducing the fundamentals of LPM, or by bolstering existing functions to incorporate process improvements and to support Knowledge Management initiatives. Featuring expert analysis on the form and function of LPM from leading industry experts, and case studies from top law firms on effective implementation and take-up, this title offers a robust overview of project management functions in the legal sector.

Jim Hassett, founder of LegalBizDev, opens the book with a discussion on why it is so important for firms to utilize legal project management as soon as possible. Referencing a study by Altman Weil, Hassett points to the three trends that clients seem to be looking for; greater cost reduction, improved budget forecasting, and non-hourly based pricing structures – and then explains how the slow pace of law firms' uptake of legal project management is failing to meet these demands.

Chapter 2 moves on to outline the basic principles of legal project management, and the processes involved in managing projects. Together

Barbara Boake, senior partner and national practice leader at McCarthy Tétrault LLP, and Rick Kathuria, national director of project management and legal logistics at Gowling WLG, define what a "project" constitutes, the differences between project management and process improvement, and the "three constraints" of scope, time, and cost; three interlinked variables that affect all projects. Chapter 3 then features Rick Kathuria and Manju Jessa, assistant general counsel at RBC General Counsel Group, offering an expert analysis on legal project management, and why many firms' futures will involve and be dependent on it. Three models of LPM are also proposed; a self-managed model, a project management office-based model, and a model based on the support of PSLs.

Chapter 4 features Lann Wasson, associate director of legal project management at Husch Blackwell LLP, discussing the "Client Value Perspective"; exploring how a firm can think strategically about delivering a service that clients deem valuable. Using the Association of Corporate Council's "Value Champions" program as hallmark of correct practice, Wasson outlines the four "rules of thumb" (as presented by Fred Gluck, founder of McKinsey's Strategy Practice) of driving value in service.

In chapter 5, Zena Applebaum, director of competitive intelligence at Bennett Jones LLP, gives an overview of how LPM and e-discovery software tie into the broader scope of business intelligence, and how the two fields can work in tandem to create, collate, and organize date to form a solid client-driven project plan. Following on from this, Lann Wasson returns in chapter 6 discussing how effective LPM initiatives can create valuable knowledge for a firm to utilize for a competitive advantage – and how the formalization of activity flow that occurs with LPM lends itself well to the creation of consistent and clear firm-wide communication, and the collection and analysis of lessons learned.

In chapter 7 Anthony Smith, founder of Legal Project Management Limited, continues the discussion of the relationship between legal project management and knowledge management with an overview of how KM staff can aid LPM operations. Smith explains how LPM should be reframed to move away from the view of it as an isolated operation – championing the multi-disciplinary approach – and how support from senior managers should be secured early to help the spread of firm-wide uptake.

Catherine Alman MacDonagh, CEO and founder of the Legal Lean Sigma Institute LLC, introduces a multi-disciplinary approach in chapter 8, outlining the fundamental differences between process improvement and project management – and what ultimately connects them. Case studies are then offered to showcase the benefits of a employing both PI and PM together (the "Multiplier Effect"), and how they can lead to significant competitive advantages.

This title then rounds off with the last section featuring case studies from leading law firms that have successfully implemented legal project management into their day-to-day functions.

Chapter 9 features Helen Bunker, divisional director of private law at Blake Morgan LLP, outlining how former firm Piper Smith Watton overcame the skepticism that fee-earners held concerning a new case management system, and how the firm ultimately increased the uptake of it throughout the firm by carefully considering the flexibility of the software, and by continually supporting development and engagement with fee-earners.

In chapter 10, Karen Dalton, senior enterprise project manager, and John Duggan, senior legal project manager at Seyfarth Shaw, offer a case study of how the implementation of LPM positively impacted client services at Seyfarth Shaw – the Seyfarth Lean initiative helped reduce "ramp up" times for all projects, improve the effectiveness of communications firm-wide, and increase the overall quality of work product. The case study also outlines the principles of Seyfarth Lean's agile project management and the challenges it faced during implementation – and also gives an overview of the lessons learned through this approach.

About the authors

Zena Applebaum is the director of competitive intelligence at Bennett Jones LLP, an international law firm based in Canada. Zena's primary responsibilities include business and practice development, market and competitor performance analysis, client relationship management, counter-intelligence, and marketing. Zena brings a unique perspective to intelligence as a result of broad business development, data management, marketing, and corporate research experience in a variety of sectors. Zena has a joint academic and applied Master of Arts degree in Communication and Culture from York and Ryerson Universities. A regular speaker, writer, and blogger on competitive intelligence topics in Canada and abroad, Zena authored *Business Intelligence for Law Firms*, published in November 2012, by the ARK Group. Zena is a sessional instructor at the University of Toronto iSchool, recently served as the chair of the SLA Competitive Intelligence Division Board of Directors, and is a former member of the SCIP Board of Directors. She can be reached at @ZAppleCI.

Catherine Alman MacDonagh, JD, is a Legal Lean Sigma Black Belt and a certified Six Sigma Green Belt. A former corporate counsel, Catherine is well known for her thought leadership and successes as a law firm executive. Now a highly-rated speaker and consultant, she works with professional services firms to create competitive advantages and organizational transformation through the development, planning, and implementation of innovative strategies, process improvement projects, and business development training and coaching programs.

Catherine is an adjunct faculty at Suffolk Law School and at George Washington University (Master's in Law Firm Management). She is also the chief enthusiasm officer of The Legal Mocktail, an experiential networking training program, and has her own consulting practice, FIRM Guidance. She is a co-founder of the Legal Sales and Service Organization. Catherine is co-author of two books: *The Woman Lawyer's*

Rainmaking Game and *The Law Firm Associate's Guide to Personal Marketing and Selling Skills*.

Barbara J. Boake is a senior partner and national practice leader at McCarthy Tétrault LLP, practicing in the areas of bankruptcy, insolvency, and restructuring. With over 20 years of practice experience and having served on her firm's board of partners and its executive team, Barbara was named one of the "Top 100 Most Powerful Women" in Canada by the Women's Executive Network. A member of her firm's executive team, she was responsible for leading the development and implementation of the firm's "Dialogue Project Management™" programme. Barbara can be contacted via email at McCarthy Tétrault LLP.

Helen Bunker is divisional director of private law at Blake Morgan LLP. Formerly managing partner of Piper Smith Watton LLP, Helen took her firm through a merger with Top 50 firm Blake Morgan in August 2015. In her new role, she leads the firm's Private Law division with responsibility for private client, residential property, and family law. Helen also has a role on the board of Blake Morgan with responsibility for both strategic vision and operational delivery. A private client lawyer by background, an MBA in Law Firm Management from Nottingham Law School in 2005 was the motivator to focus on management and leadership.

Karen Dalton is a senior project manager at Seyfarth Shaw and has over 15 years of project management experience. Ms. Dalton is responsible for implementing complex, interdepartmental, enterprise-wide, high profile technology, and process improvement projects. Ms. Dalton is well-versed in various project management methodologies, especially the agile approach.

Ms. Dalton obtained her Project Management Professional (PMP) certification from the Project Management Institute in 2005 and became a Certified ScrumMaster in 2010. She is a member of the Project Management Institute (PMI), International Legal Technology Association (ILTA), and the Scrum Alliance.

John Duggan is a senior legal project manager with SeyfarthLean Consulting. In his role, he works on a variety of firm-wide, interdepartmental, and cross-functional projects, including legal process mapping, client/attorney case management improvement, and other internal and external SeyfarthLean initiatives. Mr. Duggan has managed several complex litigation matters, large-scale FLSA audits, and declaration campaigns for firm clients. In addition, he has led the onboarding of a large trademark portfolio and managed enterprise-wide projects, such as upgrading the firm's external facing website, telephone system upgrades for all offices, and the selection and implementation of the firm's Human Resource Information System.

Mr. Duggan has over 15 years' experience as a project manager, is a certified Six Sigma Green Belt and Lean Six Sigma Black Belt, certified Agile ScrumMaster, and a certified Project Management Professional. He is also an active member of the Chicagoland Chapter of the Project Management Institute (PMI). Mr. Duggan has served as chapter president (2000) and recently completed a two-year term as vice president of Education. Mr. Duggan teaches project management courses for DeVry University and Keller Graduate School of Management.

Jim Hassett is the founder of LegalBizDev, which helps law firms increase profitability by improving project management, business development, and alternative fees. Before he started working with lawyers, Jim had 20 years of experience as a sales trainer and consultant to companies from American Express to Zurich Financial Services. He is the author of 13 books, including *The Legal Project Management Quick Reference Guide*; *Legal Project Management, Pricing, and Alternative Fee Arrangements*; *Client Value and Law Firm Profitability*; and *The Legal Business Development Quick Reference Guide*. He has also published more than 80 articles in the *New York Times Magazine*; *Bloomberg Law*; *Of Counsel*; *Legal Management*; *Strategies: The Journal of Legal Marketing*; and other publications. Jim is a frequent speaker at law firms and at bar associations (including the New York City Bar, the New York State Bar, and the Massachusetts Bar), Harvard Law School; the Association of Corporate Counsel; the Defense Research Institute; the ARK Group; and at Legal Marketing Association meetings in Boston, New York, Philadelphia, Washington, Savannah, and Vancouver. He has conducted webinars through the ARK Group; West LegalEdcenter; the National Law Journal; The International Lawyers Network; TAG Academy; and the Legal Marketing Association. Jim writes the blog *Legal Business Development* which was featured at the ABA TECHSHOW (in its list of "60 Sites: Latest and Greatest Internet Hits") and by *TechnoLawyer* (in its list of "the most influential legal blogs" in BlawgWorld). He received his Ph.D. in psychology from Harvard University.

Manju Jessa is assistant general counsel and head of the International Wealth Management legal team at RBC General Counsel Group.

Rick Kathuria is national director of project management and Legal Logistics, at Gowling WLG. In this role, he leads the firm's business transformation agenda and legal project management strategy, applying process optimization and project management principles to the delivery of sophisticated legal services. Rick is a certified project management professional (PMP), certified management consultant (CMC), and professional engineer (P.Eng.) with years of experience working on large international projects at top-tier consulting firms.

In 2011, Rick co-authored the book *Project Management for Lawyers* (ARK Group). He is a Fellow of the College of Law Practice Management and regularly coaches lawyers at law firms and in-house counsel on Legal Project Management principles and techniques. He also teaches Legal Project and Practice Management to the next generation of lawyers at the Law School at the University of Calgary.

Antony Smith is a non-practicing solicitor with post-graduate level qualifications in law, project management, and computing. Antony is a member of the Association for Project Management (MAPM), and the Project Management Institute (PMI). He is Prince II qualified (Practitioner level) and a Legal Project Practitioner (LPP). He has enjoyed project based roles at Pinsent Masons, School of Law Kings College London, Berrymans Lace Mawer, and Axxia/LexisNexis, where he spent just over 10 years in the role of strategic project manager.

Antony started his commercial career during the first wave of legal AI as a legal expert system developer. He has since successfully managed project support for complex international commercial disputes, the use of computers in courtrooms, and the implementation of practice management and workflow systems in a wide range of law firms. Antony has been called a 'completion expert' and during his career he has implemented many legal support projects which have been innovative and strategically important to the sponsoring organization.

Antony is the founder of Legal Project Management Limited (www.legalprojectmanagement.co.uk), which provides project management training and consultancy services to law firms. A practicing project manager, familiar with the challenges and opportunities available to professionals working in the legal services industry, Antony's training tends to be workshop based and reflective of the continued pressure on lawyers to "do more with less".

Lann Wasson is the associate director of legal project management at Husch Blackwell LLP and both a certified Project Management Professional and Lean Six Sigma Green Belt. For the past 16 years he has worked closely with client teams and practice groups to develop their capabilities to utilize technology, knowledge management, and legal project management approaches. Lann has worked closely with the director of legal project management and strategic pricing to develop the firm's LPM standards and trains lawyers in the firm's LPM workshops. Over the years, he has also had a number of opportunities to meet with in-house counsel and discuss how to adapt the firm's technology platforms to their needs as well as suggest how knowledge management and legal project management could augment law department programs and strategies. Lann can be reached at lann.wasson@huschblackwell.com.

Chapter 1: Why is it urgent to implement LPM?

By Jim Hassett, founder of LegalBizDev

The primary reason that it is urgent to implement Legal Project Management (LPM) is simple: clients want it.

For the last several years, in its annual *Chief Legal Officers Survey*, Altman Weil has listed 10 top trends and asked, "Of the following service improvements and innovations, please select the three you would most like to see from your outside counsel."[1] The list includes preventative law strategies, improved communication, alternative project staffing, and technology efficiencies. The top three in the most recent (2016) survey were:

- Greater cost reduction (selected by 53 percent of respondents);
- Improved budget forecasting (43 percent); and
- Non-hourly based pricing structures (36 percent).

Since LPM leads directly to #1 and #2 and is very important for success in #3, you could sum up the results by saying that what clients want most these days is LPM, LPM, and more LPM.

Law firms are moving slowly

How well are law firms doing in meeting this client need? Not very well. When CLOs were asked, "In your opinion, in the current legal market, how serious are law firms about changing their legal service delivery model to provide greater value to clients (as opposed to simply cutting costs)?" on a scale from 0 to 10, the median rating (with half the firms above and half below) was 3. This median value has been identical for the five years the survey asked the question (2012–2016), so despite all the press releases law firms are putting out trumpeting their successes in increasing value, clients have not been impressed by the results.

Turning to the law firm perspective, the first question in Altman Weil's 2016 *Law Firms in Transition Survey* was, "Which of the following legal market trends do you think are temporary and which will be permanent?" The top three answers were more price competition (95 percent think this is permanent), focus on improved practice efficiency (93 percent), and more commoditized legal work (88 percent).[2] Of course, all three can be addressed through LPM.

But when Altman Weil asked the same group, "Has your firm significantly changed its strategic approach to efficiency of legal service delivery?" only 44 percent said yes (26 percent said no and 30 percent said changes were "under consideration"). Summing this up, 93 percent of firm leaders think more efficiency is needed, but only 44 percent are doing something about it. What's wrong with this picture?

In many cases firms that say they have "changed their strategic approach" have done so only for a small sub-group within the firm or in a strategic plan which has not yet been implemented. In the trenches, the vast majority of lawyers are still practicing the way they always have. Perhaps this should not be surprising, since LPM requires lawyers to change habits they've developed over decades, and no one likes to change.[3]

The gap between what firms should be doing and what they are actually doing has existed for years. Fortunately, the survey dug into the details of what's behind the problem. Authors Eric Seeger and Tom Clay concluded; "The biggest impediment to change, identified by 64 percent of law firm leaders, is that partners resist most change efforts."[4] As a long-term strategy in a profession where client demands are changing rapidly, that's a great way to insure that your job will be in danger.

In 1962, Professor Everett Rogers analyzed the forces involved in changing business behavior and summarized his conclusions in an influential text entitled *Diffusion of Innovations*, which is now in its fifth edition. In this context, the most important idea is his argument that the people who adopt a new idea are distributed in a normal curve in several sequential categories, which he called innovators (2.5 percent), early adopters (13.5 percent), early majority (34 percent), late majority (34 percent), and laggards (16 percent).

While it is impossible to prove exactly where LPM stands on this continuum, based on our experience talking to a wide number of firms, we strongly believe that LPM is at the early adopters' stage. A small group of innovators has successfully proven its value, but the spread to others remains slow. Many law firms have done an excellent job at putting out press releases announcing that they are leaders in LPM, but when it comes to changing the way an entire practice group or firm does business, they have fallen far short.

If you believed what you read on the internet, you'd think that LPM had already swept the legal profession and that a large number of firms have developed a solid track record of success. However, it is an open secret among people in the field that there is a huge gap between the success that many firms claim on their web pages and the slow pace of LPM adoption within even the most vocal firms.

Even the firms that have been most serious about making this change have found that progress is slow. Seyfarth Shaw is one of the best known names in LPM and has been working aggressively on implementing it for more than a decade. But the firm's chair and managing partner Steven Poor has written in the *New York Times Dealbook* blog that one should "Never underestimate lawyers' resistance to change."[5] That's the bad news. The good news was summarized by Lisa Damon, the partner who leads Seyfarth*Lean*, who has said that, "If you get a group of lawyers and staff into a room to discuss how to make things more efficient, it's very easy to find savings."[6]

When you put these two facts together – it's easy to figure out how to be efficient, but hard to get lawyers to act on it – you begin to see why there is so much confusion about what works best for LPM and about which firms have made the most progress. Add in the vested interest that firms have in publicizing any success they do achieve, the fact that there are wide individual differences between lawyers within a single firm, and secrecy within firms, and it becomes clear that it is almost impossible for outsiders to compare firms on their progress.

The bad news here is that clients want faster progress. The good news is that to win new business you just have to be a little better than your competitors, so law firms that have started down the LPM path have an enormous opportunity to get ahead of those who have not.

Glacial progress can produce new business when you are competing with firms that are making no progress at all. We were reminded of this when one client contacted us two years after we offered just-in-time LPM coaching at her firm. She reported that they had just won some new business as a result of using LPM. She went on to say that she had been frustrated by the slow pace of change in her firm, but in this case it did not matter because their competitors were even slower. "If you move like a turtle but you're racing a bunch of snails," she said, "it all works out in the end."

The slow rate of progress is in some ways hard to understand given the potential payoffs. As Altman Weil put it in one survey:

Perhaps no other long-term initiative will do more to support staffing innovation, pricing innovation, efficient delivery of services, improvements in margin, and reductions in overhead than true project management training. It's important to distinguish between a one- or two-day seminar which will not produce much long-term value, and a systematic, hands-on approach that instills fundamental operational change. Firms that give their people the right kind of tools and training in this area will create new efficiencies for clients, improve profitability of matters, and create significant competitive advantage.[7]

LPM benefits

When I interviewed managing partners, chairs, and other leaders of 50 AmLaw 200 firms for my book *Client Value and Law Firm Profitability*, several talked about the importance of implementing LPM:

One of the problems that we have, and frankly that most firms have, is just teaching lawyers how to manage a project, getting them out of the habit of just automatically starting out with some rote process. Just because the client says "I think I might have a lawsuit" doesn't mean you go off and conduct 40 depositions. Lawyers need to sit down and talk about what the client is trying to accomplish. It might turn out that we are able to accomplish the client's end goal without taking any depositions.

Most of our clients are no better at understanding or applying legal project management than we are. But in the future, the fact that you can actually do something on time and within budget is going to become an important indicator of whether or not you really are a good lawyer.

If you apply all its principles, LPM is not that scary, and it's not that hard. Just getting people to understand it and do it is the biggest challenge.[8]

According to an ALM Intelligence survey, firms that have begun to apply LPM, even in very limited ways, have already received benefits. When the survey asked "Which of the following 13 benefits has your firm realized from its project management effort?" every single benefit in their list had been realized by at least 20 percent of the group. The most common benefit was "More productive relationships with clients" (achieved by 62 percent).

The ALM survey concluded that:

LPM can help bring increased effectiveness, reduce wasted time, and manage client expectations... Law firms can overcome [the] hurdles by targeting initial efforts in areas that would be most receptive, incrementally rolling out initiatives, and getting experienced help. Those that can successfully implement LPM will find over time that they gain a competitive advantage.[9]

In our research on *Client Value and Law Firm Profitability*, 85 percent of law firm leaders said that firms that move more quickly in providing value will gain a competitive advantage. Several respondents described this as a matter of life and death:

I think the firms that are most effective are going to do well, and I don't think everybody will survive. In the last several years, there have been several firms that went away. And I believe that's going to continue.

The way law firms deliver legal services to clients is undergoing a huge revolution. It's going to change before our eyes in the course of a very short period of time. And it's all being driven by clients who want to get value for their money.

I think the market's going to shake itself out. I think firms that can't deliver more value will fail.[10]

As the chair of another firm summed it up:

I believe that we're still in the beginning of the process. There are a number of famous economists who have talked about disruptive technologies and disruptive business processes. I think there's a lot of evidence out there that this profession is being subjected to those pressures. Five years from now, if I turn out to be wrong, that will be great. But if I'm right, then I have to believe that those firms that adapt more quickly will have a competitive advantage, because the firms that don't adapt quickly enough will be out of business.[11]

Defining LPM broadly

Despite the clear need for LPM, there is still some confusion about exactly how to define the term. Of course, project management has long been used by other businesses to protect profits through predictability and efficiency. Their projects – from the design and production of a new line of jet engines to the acquisition and integration of a billion-dollar company – can reach nearly unimaginable levels of complexity, variability, and risk. Professions from engineering to investment banking have developed a rich and deep body of knowledge about how to manage projects on time and within budget. Legal project management adapts these proven techniques to the unique challenges of managing unpredictable legal matters and disputes.

By our definition *legal project management increases client satisfaction and firm profitability by applying proven techniques to improve the management of legal matters.* Thus, we see LPM as an umbrella term that embraces a very wide range of management techniques, including pricing, communication, process improvement, and much more. It can be further broken down into the eight key issues listed in Table 1.

Key Issue	**Description**
Set objectives and define scope	You must define your assumptions and specify exactly what is included in the assignment and what is not. It is often useful to specify certain important things that are not included.
Identify and schedule activities	After scope is clearly defined, break down a complex matter into smaller tasks and schedule them.
Assign tasks and manage the team	To maximize efficiency, the right people must be assigned to the right tasks, team members must understand the project's scope and their responsibilities, and performance must be monitored.
Plan and manage the budget	Estimating and controlling costs are a challenge in every profession, and this is the most critical area for many lawyers.
Assess risks to the budget and schedule	What can you do at the beginning of a matter to mitigate risks and increase the chances that work will be completed on time, within budget?
Manage quality	Most lawyers are very good at delivering high quality legal work. However, this becomes more challenging when schedules change and budgets get reduced.
Manage client communication and expectations	This is extremely important to clients and it is an area where many lawyers have room to improve. This section describes best practices, including using a "RACI matrix" to clarify who is Responsible, Accountable, Consulted, and Informed for each task.
Negotiate changes of scope	No matter how well lawyers manage legal matters, things often change. The issue here is deciding when and how to negotiate these changes with clients.

Table 1: Eight key issues in LPM

Others disagree. For example, the field of knowledge management (KM) identifies useful intellectual property created during past matters and then leverages that knowledge inside the firm through increased access and sharing. In some firms, LPM and KM are entirely separate departments. In others, LPM staff are part of the KM department or KM staff are part of the LPM department.

If a management technique can help lawyers accomplish their goals, we say it is part of LPM. We believe that hair splitting over what is and is not LPM can become just another excuse to avoid action. Law firms need to move as quickly as possible to the central problem addressed by LPM: What must we do today to meet client needs while remaining profitable?

Another example: personal time management is not mentioned in many project management courses and texts, nor is it listed in the index of the Project Management Institute's *Guide to the Project Management Body of Knowledge*, the bible of the field which is used to certify project managers in other industries. But for some lawyers, personal time management is a vitally important skill which can increase value and profitability. When we coach lawyers in LPM, it is often the first topic they need to focus on.

Like Barbara Boake and Rick Kathuria, the authors of *Project Management for Lawyers*, we believe that "project management is a tool box – choose only what you need to most effectively manage [each] project."[12] The key to success is to find the "low-hanging fruit," the management tactics that are most likely to help each individual to increase value and/or profitability.

By our definition, any lawyer who has ever planned a budget or managed a team has served as a legal project manager. But what was "good project management" for lawyers a few years ago is no longer good enough. Clients are now choosing law firms based on their ability to apply a more systematic and disciplined approach that delivers more value more quickly.

While there is widespread agreement that clients want LPM and that it pays off for firms, the field is so new that experts still disagree about exactly what should be included and excluded from its definition. These arguments have slowed LPM's progress, as seen in the remarks of this AmLaw 200 firm leader from our *Client Value* survey:

> *We were just at a board meeting last week where we were talking about whether we should do formalized project management training. My answer to that is obviously yes, we absolutely should. But first we need to agree on what legal project management is.*[13]

I first became aware of the seriousness of this problem a few years ago when the director of professional development at an AmLaw 100 firm asked me to explain the differences between project management, process improvement, Six Sigma, and Lean. This was an extremely sophisticated client who had been researching this area for months, but she had heard so many different claims from competing consultants that she had trouble keeping them straight.

Process improvement, Six Sigma, and Lean have gotten a lot of headlines in the legal world as a result of Seyfarth Shaw's highly publicized success in using them to streamline work. All three approaches originated in the world of manufacturing.

Six Sigma is built around techniques Motorola developed to eliminate the causes of manufacturing defects and errors. Lean was developed by Toyota to increase manufacturing efficiency by eliminating the "seven wastes" (excess inventory, excess processing, overproduction, transportation, motion, waiting, and defects).

Process improvement typically starts by defining the exact steps that are required to perform a legal process. This includes looking at every process from the client's point of view, analyzing whether each step adds value for the client, and eliminating the steps that don't.

Writing in *Law Technology*, Alan Cohen has noted that this traditional approach "can take weeks to create a map, but the result is a template that spells out the various phases of a matter – and an efficient way to do them."[14] If you consider the fact that Seyfarth has developed over 500 process maps, each of which took a team of lawyers and staff weeks to develop, you can see why *Six Sigma for Dummies* says the approach is "not for the faint of heart. It is intense and rigorous, and it entails a thorough inspection of the way everything is done."[15]

In my book, *Legal Project Management, Pricing and Alternative Fee Arrangements*, I described how Seyfarth has spent more than 10 years and millions of dollars refining its system. They have trademarked the term Seyfarth*Lean* and formed a separate company – Seyfarth*Lean*® Consulting – as a wholly owned subsidiary which offers advice to law departments on how to work more efficiently.

Given our broad definition of LPM, you will not be surprised to learn that we consider process improvement, Six Sigma, and Lean to be specialized approaches that fall under the more general umbrella term LPM. They are simply tools in the belt, to be used in some cases and ignored in others. And when they are used, we recommend always looking for simpler and more efficient approaches.

This article was adapted with permission from the fourth edition of the Legal Project Management Quick Reference Guide *(copyright 2016, LegalBizDev). For more information, see http://tinyurl.com/LPMbook or call 800-49-TRAIN.*

References

1. Altman Weil, "Chief Legal Officer Survey", 2016. See: http://www.altmanweil.com/CLO2016, 26.
2. Altman Weil, "Law Firms in Transition Survey", 2016. See: http://www.altmanweil.com/LFiT2016/, 1.
3. I spend my life talking to law firm leaders about what they are doing to increase efficiency, and my guess is that the percent of firms that have made significant changes is closer to four percent than to 44%.
4. See reference 2.
5. Poor, S., "Re-Engineering the Business of Law", *New York Times Dealbook* 2012. See: http://dealbook.nytimes.com/2012/05/07/re-engineering-the-business-of-law/
6. Hasset, J., "Alternative fess (part 3): What your competitors are doing", 2009. See: http://adverselling.typepad.com/how_law_firms_sell/2009/01/alternative-fees-part-3-what-your-competitors-are-doing.html.
7. Altman Weil, "Law Firms in Transition Survey", 2014. See: http://www.altmanweil.com/dir_docs/resource/f68236ab-d51f-4d81-8172-96e8d47387e3_document.pdf.
8. Hassett, J., *Client Value and Law Firm Profitability*, LegalBizDev, 2013.
9. ALM Legal Intelligence, "Alternative Fee Arrangements at Legal Departments and Law Firms", 2015. See: http://www.almlegalintel.com/SurveyDescription.aspx?id=VSLYO4Oih00=&type=fEFglaD+grg=, 17
10. See reference 8.
11. ibid.
12. Boake, B., and Kathuria, R., *Project Management for Lawyers*, London, ARK Group, 2011.
13. See reference 8.
14. Cohen, A., "How six big law firms gets serious about legal project management", 2013. See: http://www.dailyreportonline.com/id=1202566995546/How-six-big-law-firms-get-serious-about-legal-project-management.
15. Gig, C., Decal, N., and Covey, S.R., *Six Sigma for Dummies*, Wiley Publishing, 2005.

Chapter 2: Project management foundational principles

By Barbara J. Boake, national practice leader at McCarthy Terrault, and Rick Kathuria, national director of project management at Gowling WLG

It is helpful to gain a foundation in project management theory before applying the tools and techniques to a legal practice. This chapter provides an explanation of basic project management principles and the people and processes involved in managing projects.

What is project management?

Project management is a structured approach to planning and managing projects. It is a recognized discipline with a standard set of skills, tools, and techniques used across all industries. It began its evolution as a distinct profession in the 1950s as organizations started to systematically apply project management techniques to complex engineering projects.[1] As project managers became more experienced, a body of knowledge developed into a set of standards described in A Guide to the Project Management Body of Knowledge (PMBOK® Guide).[2] The legal project management framework described in this report is based to a large extent on the PMBOK® Guide.

There is a wide variety of recognized project management tools and techniques that have been used for decades, primarily by engineering and information technology professionals. The key to introducing project management to lawyers is to adopt only those principles that will be useful in a legal practice and, above all, to make it simple. The discussion of project management in this report focuses on those tools and techniques that are simple and useful enough to be embraced by a busy practicing lawyer.

Although project management has been used with success for years in other disciplines, the complex and adversarial nature of legal work is seen to be ill-suited to a standard set of rote management processes. More fundamentally, lawyers have difficulty characterising legal matters as projects. However, we hope it will become clear in this report that principles borrowed from the field of project management can be adapted to a legal practice with great results for both law firms and their clients.

What is a project?

A project is "a temporary endeavour undertaken to create a unique result".[3] Although the end result of a project is often intended to be permanent (a building or the acquisition of a new business), the project itself has a specific beginning and end.

A legal mandate begins when a client engages a law firm to work on a matter with a view to obtaining a desired result. The mandate ends when the result is achieved or when it becomes clear that the result is not achievable. Accordingly, there is no reason why legal matters would not benefit from practices that have been developed, tested, and used with success for years by professional project managers.

The Project Management Institute (PMI) is the leading international association for the project management profession. It provides numerous levels of professional certifications. PMI has recently given more attention to legal project management. In September 2010, PMI launched what is called a "Community of Practice" or "Virtual Community", focusing solely on legal project management. The community was launched by volunteers who had a great deal of experience or interest in this area. These volunteers formed the first executive committee for the group and are responsible for the content and operation of the site.[4]

Project management versus process management

Some law firms have looked for ways to improve efficiency in the delivery of legal services using a combination of project management and process management. The "Seyfarth*Lean*" programme developed by Seyfarth Shaw LLP is an adaptation of "Lean Six Sigma", which itself is a combination of two process management methodologies. "Six Sigma" is a rigorous methodology using data and statistical analysis to measure and improve a company's operational performance by identifying and eliminating defects in the end product of a manufacturing process.

Lean is a set of principles, concepts, and techniques designed for the elimination of waste in manufacturing processes. Both methodologies focus on finding the most efficient process by examining each task, asking whether it is necessary and finding the best process for performing it. Project management assumes that this analysis has already been completed and imposes a structure or discipline to ensure that each task is managed to completion.

The triple constraints

"A project can be good, fast, or cheap. Pick any two." This old project management adage captures the fundamental challenge faced by all project managers. Every project has three key constraints that must be considered together:

- Scope (good);
- Time (fast); and
- Cost (cheap).

These constraints are often depicted as a triangle (see Figure 1) to show the relationship between them and to highlight the fact that a change to one of the constraints will affect at least one – and often both – of the other two.

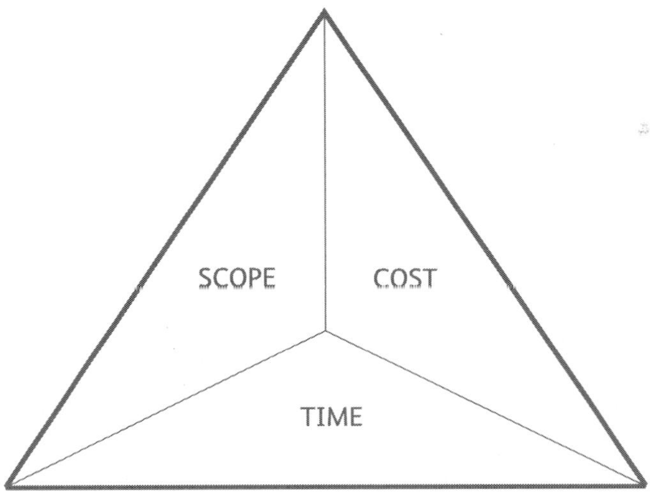

Figure 1: The "Iron Triangle"

Figure 1 is referred to by project managers as the "Iron Triangle". This is a helpful model as it highlights the interdependency of the three constraints that must operate within a rigid structure. If one side of the triangle is increased, one or both of the other sides must be manipulated as well.

For example, if unanticipated work is added to a project, the scope side of the triangle will lengthen. As the scope increases, at least one other side of the triangle must move to join it. If additional resources are added to the project in order to complete the work on the same schedule, the cost side of the triangle will lengthen, but the time side of the triangle will remain the same. This is depicted further in Figure 2.

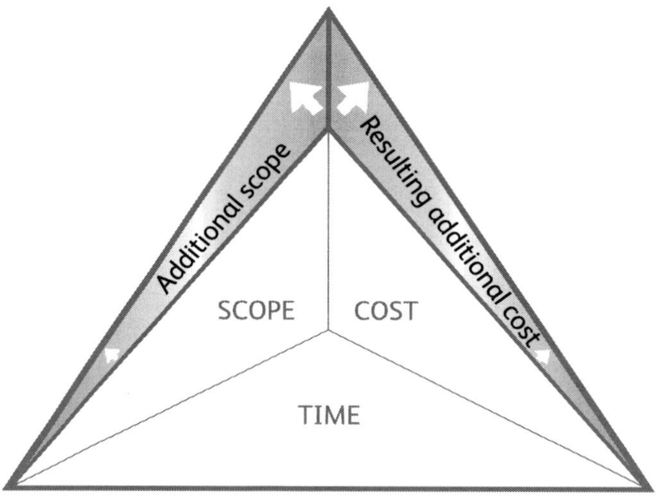

Figure 2: Increasing scope without impacting time

If no additional resources are added to the project, both the time and the cost sides of the triangle must increase proportionately. This is depicted in Figure 3.

The inverse of this is also true. If a client requests that anticipated costs be reduced, this cannot be accomplished without reducing the scope of the work. This may or may not affect the time it takes to complete the work.

Figure 4 depicts the scenario where both cost and time are reduced as a result of the request for a lower cost.

Clearly, there are more than three constraints in planning and managing projects. For example, if a client is prepared to accept more risk or a lower quality, these variables can be manipulated to achieve a lower cost or shorter timeline. (There are other project management

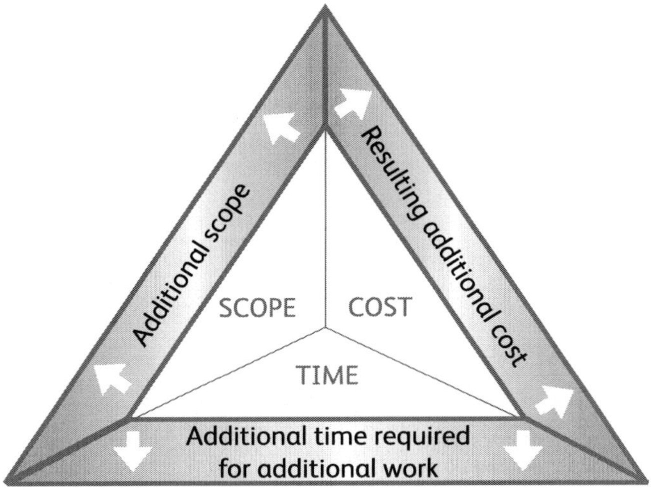

Figure 3: Consequences of adding scope

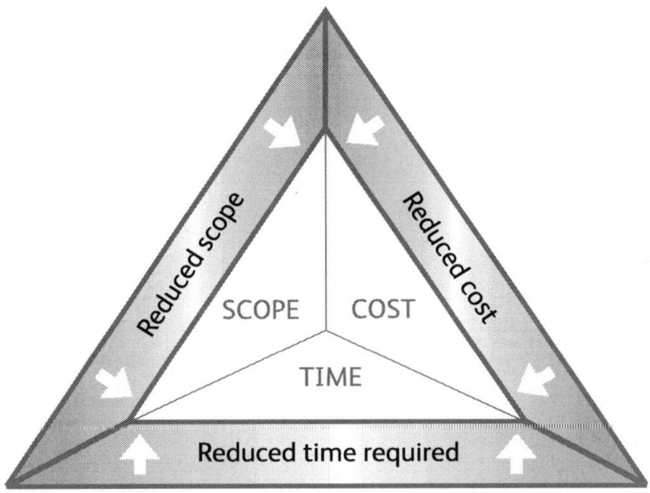

Figure 4: Consequences of reducing cost

triangles that depict these relationships and dependencies that are described in project management literature.) However, in a law firm, quality cannot be compromised and risks are typically assessed as substantive legal issues rather than as risks to a project's schedule or budget. In the context of a legal practice, quality and risk are not, strictly speaking, constraints that lend themselves easily to manipulation for the sake of better project management. For this reason, we focus on the triple constraints of scope, time, and cost as we discuss in the legal project management framework throughout this report.

The project sponsor

A project is initiated by a project sponsor. The project sponsor is the individual employed by your client who will be leading the project, providing instructions, and approving the legal fees. It is the project sponsor who has internal accountability for the project, and who must justify any cost overruns or schedule delays. After a law firm is retained on a new matter, it is of course at all times representing its client. However, in a project management model, it is sometimes useful to think of the sponsor as the individual rather than the organization. This subtle distinction is important for lawyers to keep in mind, so as to focus not only on the legal outcome but also on the client's overall experience working with its law firm.

In a legal project management framework, "client" and "sponsor" are often used interchangeably. There is no harm in this. In fact, there is a benefit to reducing jargon, particularly when introducing new initiatives to lawyers. Throughout this report, we will use both terms, using "sponsor" where it is useful to highlight the distinction between a lawyer's responsibility as legal adviser and his/her responsibility as project manager.

The project manager

The project manager is "the person assigned by the performing organization to achieve the project objectives".[5] He/she is accountable to the project sponsor for all cost overruns and schedule delays. The project manager is responsible for keeping the sponsor informed throughout the project and for resolving conflicts within the project team.

A project manager can be any member of a project team. In a legal project management framework, there could be a wide variety of individuals who qualify for this role, including non-legal support personnel. For this reason, the term "project manager" is used generically throughout this report, although we often use it interchangeably with "lawyer", particularly when providing examples or discussing project management responsibilities that are best performed by lawyers.

There are no typical personality types for project managers but the most successful exhibit the following traits:

- They must be pragmatic – although they need to understand the strategic vision and objectives of the project, they do not need to be visionaries. They must be able to focus on the details of the project without micro-managing the project team. They must be able to identify decisions that present a material risk to the project (which should be discussed with, and supported by, the project sponsor) and everyday decisions required to keep the project running efficiently. Good project managers understand that it is better to make a good decision quickly than a great decision too late.
- They should be good communicators – they do not need to be extroverts, but they do need to feel comfortable talking to people and working with a team and a sponsor to resolve issues. They must be confident enough to push back where appropriate; and
- They must remain objective – they should stay away from the blame game. As issues surface, effective project managers will raise options with the project sponsor and, in many cases, make a recommendation. Great project managers have mastered the art of negotiation and collaboration when working towards a compromise.

Project management processes

There are five key processes that contribute to the success of a project. These processes are used in all projects regardless of the particular profession or industry group for whom the project has been undertaken. They ensure the effective flow of work from beginning to end. The processes generally occur chronologically, so that output of one process generally becomes the input of another.[6] The five main processes are outlined in the following:

Process one – Initiation

This is the process of defining the desired project outcome to ensure the sponsor and the project manager agree on what is expected. At this stage, all objectives are articulated and the triple constraints of scope, time, and cost are addressed. In a legal project management model, the lead lawyer has a significant role to play in this process.

Process two – Planning

A plan is developed to achieve the desired outcome. The plan will include the tasks and resources required to complete the tasks, as well as an estimate of the cost of completing the work. A summary of the plan will be approved by the sponsor, as part of this process.

Process three – Execution

The project team completes and delivers the work. In most project management models, the project manager's role is limited to ensuring effective communication with the sponsor and within the project team. However, in a legal project management model, the project manager may also be a key member of the team with many tasks to perform.

Process four – Monitoring and controlling

This is the process of tracking and reviewing the performance of the project and identifying areas where changes to the plan have occurred, or may be required. The project manager's role is to ensure the project is progressing on budget and on time, and that the agreed-upon work is being completed. In a legal project management model, these project management responsibilities could be performed by junior lawyers or non-legal support personnel.

Process five – Closing

The formal closing of the project involves the acceptance by the sponsor of the completed work, the documentation of lessons learned on the project and the archiving of relevant documents to be used on future projects.

The project life cycle

The five project management processes are typically performed in the same sequence on all projects, regardless of the specific work involved.[7] They are depicted in the PMI's project life cycle in Figure 5.

An understanding of the concepts depicted in this project life cycle is an important starting point for lawyers using project management for the first time. If one accepts that a successfully-managed project must move through each of the processes depicted in Figure 5, regardless of the specific work involved, it is not long before a model emerges that can reduce even the most complex legal mandate into its component project parts.

The project life cycle has a circular pattern. This is because unanticipated events arising during the execution process will require a return to the planning process. The monitoring process surrounds both planning and execution since it encapsulates both. This is a helpful way to visualize legal matters which, more often than not, require many deviations from the original strategy or plan.

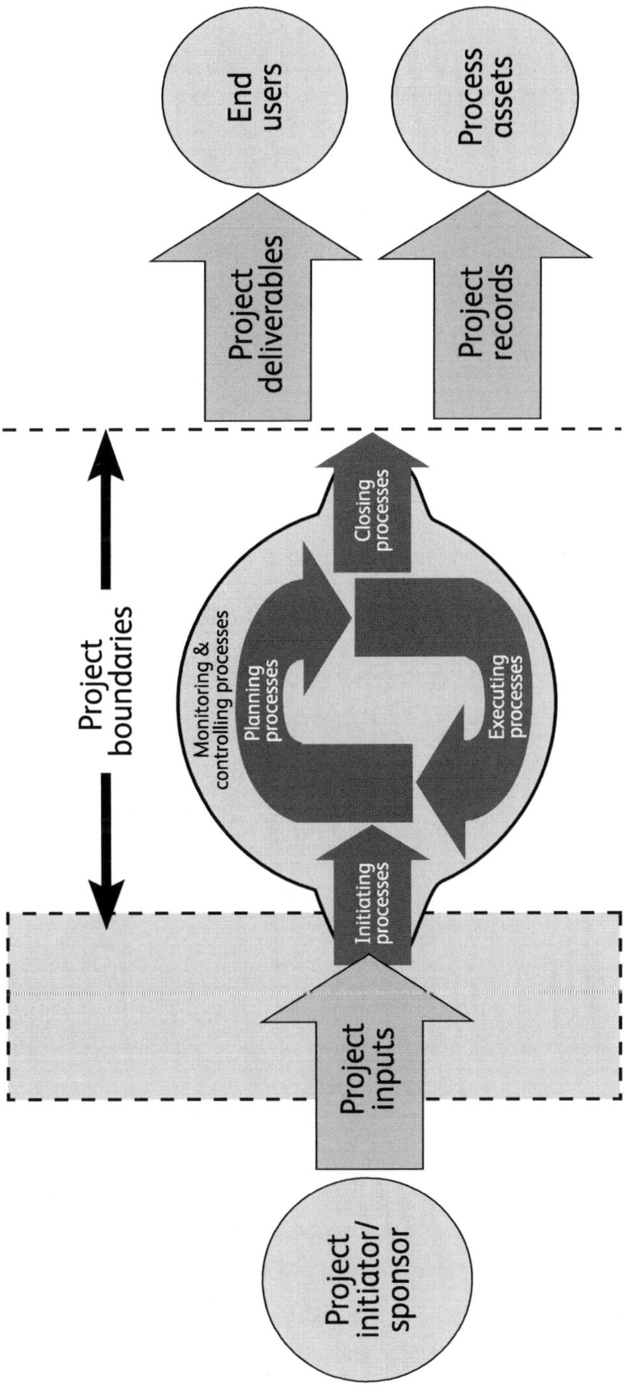

Figure 5: The PMI Project Life cycle[8]

The project boundaries that appear on either side of the circle are another key element of the model. It is critical to establish, at the beginning of a project, what is inside and what is outside these boundaries. As we will discuss in more detail in this report, unless a lawyer and client have agreed on the boundaries of the project, it will be difficult to assess whether any changes to the work are included in, or excluded from, the original fee estimate for the work.

The importance of "process assets"

As Figure 5 shows, a completed project produces two distinct end products. The first and most obvious are the "deliverables", which ultimately reside with the end user (your client). In a legal matter, this could be a completed transaction or a favourable judgment.

A less obvious end product of a project is the project records – the plans, budgets, precedents, and lessons learned from the processes used to complete the project. An effective legal project management model must provide a structure for saving these "process" assets. A thorough evaluation of a project, once it has been completed, will enable the work product to be used in the planning and execution of future projects.

A few rules to live by

In addition to understanding the foundational principles upon which the legal project management framework is built, it helps to keep a few simple rules in mind:

- Project management is a tool box – choose only what you need to most effectively manage the project. You would not reach for a calculator to add two single digit numbers, just as it is not necessary to create a detailed project plan for a few days' work;
- Plan now or pay later – a little time upfront can save a great deal of time and effort later. While it is common to hear, "I don't have time to create a plan, I need to get this done now", this is the equivalent of saying to a client, "I don't have time to work efficiently, I need to do it quickly";
- The simplest process is often the best – over-complicating project management with too many processes will increase costs and reduce efficiency without adding much real value; and
- There should be no surprises – regular and effective communication is the key to successful project management. Project managers

must stay several steps ahead of the sponsor of the project, who should never be surprised by anything that does not also surprise the project manager.

A version of this article first appeared in Boake, B. and Kathuria, R. Project Management for Lawyers, *London: ARK Group, 2011*

References

1. Carayannis, E.G, et al., *The Story of Managing Projects*, Greenwood Publishing Group, 2005.
2. *A Guide to the Project Management Body of Knowledge* (PMBOK® Guide) – Fourth Edition, Project Management Institute, Inc., 2008.
3. Ibid.
4. For more information on PMI's work on legal project management, visit PMI's website at: http:// www.pmi.org and the legal project management website at: http:// legalpm.vc.pmi.org.
5. See reference 2.
6. Ibid.
7. Ibid.
8. Ibid.

Chapter 3:
Expert analysis – Legal project management

By Rick Kathuria, director PM and Legal Logistics at Gowling WLG and a member of the University of Calgary's Law school faculty where he lectures on Legal Project Management, and Manju Jessa, Assistant General Counsel, RBC General Counsel Group

The ability to adapt is a must in order to increase one's chances of survival. The same fate lies with law firms which choose to continue on a business as usual model when the environment for delivering legal services to the client is rapidly changing. Change agents include clients requiring valuable, efficient, practical, timely, and cost effective legal service. For this reason, the business as usual model cannot and will not survive. Law firms will change in a drive to be ever more vigilant, innovative, internally efficient, and to act as trend setters themselves in order to remain competitive in the market they are facing today – and will continue to face.

Due to clients' requests to move away from hourly billing to non-standard billing models, law firms need to look internally and determine how they can operate their firms in a viable, cost efficient, and client focused manner. The traditional law firm will need to move towards the positive end of the spectrum of a value-based business model. High-end clients will not necessarily seek out the low cost provider, but provide more of their legal business to a provider that provides high value and meets the buyer's intrinsic needs. For example, take Harrods or Whole Foods. Both are high-end stores open to the general public. But who actually shops there? Clients who are seeking value, rather than low price, are their loyal returning customers.

In today's business environment, organizations have objectives particularly where shareholders are concerned. The objectives typically require employees to be cost efficient in external procurement, which includes the in-house lawyer or business person who is the buyer of law firm legal services. The cost efficiency is measured through somehow demonstrating how much the in-house lawyer or business person will save in the coming year, how they perform against their target forecast budget, and the change in their budget year over year. Clients will seek out help to deliver these savings-related targets from the law firms they partner with. A client will always drive business to whoever can make them look good and be loyal to law firms which operate in a manner that can help them meet their own objectives. Therefore, the senior leadership teams of law firms will need to acknowledge that clients will shift to law firms that not only provide excellent legal services, but are seen to be helping the client to meet their internal deliverable.

Law firms are also receiving increased inquiries into their mapping and processes of completing a legal mandate from start to finish. To this day, the necessary level of predictability and visibility during the life of a law firm delivering a legal mandate is often below a client's expectation. This in turn leads to uncertain fees which in turn lead clients to successfully negotiate fixed fees just so they are certain about the spend. These fixed fees also help align a client's need with that of the law firm. Efficient and effective delivery of work. For the firms that are providing fixed fees, the client is typically billed on regular time-based intervals or based on the delivery of specific outputs or at key events in the mandate. In these situations, clients are not impacted by overages in actual time accrued since it will not impact the negotiated fixed fee unless there was a change in the scope of work. Even without fixed fees, many clients are already stating that they will not pay for any legal services above the specified budget unless the change was approved in advance of the work being performed.

All of the above-mentioned points that clients value lead to at least one principle. What law firms will need to put high on their leadership's agenda is to enable the firm to demonstrate to its clients the proven ability of time management and project management. Accordingly, the law firm of the future will include, in some shape or form, legal project management.

Not only will legal project management enable the firm to survive in this environment and potentially bring to its door new clients who are migrating from their traditional law firm providers, it will assist the law firm internally to evolve by enabling it to meet the needs of its staff, in particular junior lawyers, paralegals, support staff, and clerks. Project management will bear fruit to the law firm if a firm trains its staff in this much needed area. Part of the benefit of project management is its ability to provide the entire legal project team with the strategy of how the work is to be done and by when. In a business as usual law firm, typically, the senior partner will simply talk to their senior associate about the legal mandate regarding what needs to be done. A written record of this was typically not created and therefore a project plan was typically neglected. But a firm which integrates legal project management into its everyday practice will create the project plan and share it with the entire legal team delivering the work on the matter. The sharing of this plan will in itself provide the entire team with a holistic view of the why, what, who, where, and when picture on the legal mandate the firm is to execute. The sharing of this plan will connect each of the legal team members to one another and enable the team to be fully engaged, perform at a higher rate, and become very efficient. The team will know their work and the budget/time allotted to do the work. Each lawyer on that team will be stretched, challenged, and highly engaged to the point where at the end of the mandate, the junior lawyers will have experienced a steep learning curve because work is assigned at the appropriate level based on a thoughtful approach to the staffing of the mandate. The project plan, the sharing, and delivery on the project plan will actually create better business focused and practical lawyers.

What exactly the implementation will look like will vary from law firm to law firm, but there will generally be three models:

1. **Self-managed** – Projects are self-managed by the legal team undertaking the work;
2. **Project management office** – Projects are managed with the help of non-lawyers who are project managers but sit on the services side within the law firm; and
3. **Professional support lawyers** – Projects are managed with the help of a lawyer acting purely in a support capacity and not responsible for delivering the legal mandate.

In all of these models, there will need to be direct access to financial information for the matter by the team. The expected influx of volume of requests for financial reporting will not make it feasible to mandate that the finance department deliver ad-hoc reporting to financial progress on the matter. As such, firms will find ways to provide this information readily available as needed in an easy manner. In the long term, this "near" real-time financial information will also be readily available directly to clients. This need will be driven by the law firm wanting to demonstrate its competitive advantage. While the specific buyers of legal services will likely not be the driver for this, it will probably come through as a competitive differentiator through the request for proposal (RFP) process as an offering by a law firm. As a result of this near real-time access to the information, this will also lead firms to move closer towards near real-time entry for professional staff. The reason for near-real time is because there is often some review that needs to happen during the process such as some time to be written off. Some firms will accept this and provide real time access while others may opt for a near-real time view.

Let's examine how each of these models works with some of the benefits and drawbacks of each.

Self-managed

Projects self-managed by the legal team undertaking the work

This model is similar to the way the majority of law firms in their infancy of legal project management operate today, with one big difference. The difference will be the regular reporting on the WIP to senior management and client relationship managers on a portfolio basis with visibility into progress against budget on key high value, high risk, and/or key client mandates. Nothing strengthens a relationship manager's rapport with a client than to know of a client's potential concern and to address it proactively. Law firms that are not already doing this will soon see enough value to implement this quick win.

In the short term, this will be the predominate form of legal project management. The benefit of this is that it is easy to implement and requires only a modest change for those firms who are not already doing this. The structure of the team will not really change, but the project management responsibilities will be borne by the project team. In this model, it is possible that the legal assistant will be responsible for pulling reports from the project management or financial system and provide them to the billing lawyer at predetermined intervals. The project plan itself will be documented or at the very least a high-level plan with a budget. Firms will generally work with budgets at the phase level.

The advantage of this model is its simplicity. Most law firms already work this way. Therefore, to layer some project management administrative requirements on top of the existing work will not be a significant behavioural change, particularly if it is to be executed by lower cost resources such as legal secretaries or very junior timekeepers.

The disadvantage of this model is that it leaves itself open to individual preferences on the way the work is done. For this reason, it will not provide a consistent experience to clients of the law firm. Also, this model may not be viewed as a long-term investment in the growth of the law firm. This model also makes it very easy for lawyers who do not want to do it continue with the status quo.

Law firms which have not yet embarked on any form of legal project management will probably utilize this model as the first step on their legal project management journey. Why? Because the benefits of the subtle change will allow the employees of the law firm to see the value and will hopefully drive the law firm towards more legal project management capabilities and better processes.

Project management office

Projects managed with the help of non-lawyers who are project managers but sit on the administrative side within the law firm

In this model, there will initially be an additional resource added to the mandate. Essentially, a project manager who may be PMP certified and would typically work in a non-billing role. The project manager will be responsible for providing the project management capabilities to the legal team on each new work matter. The project manager will enable the legal team to deliver the matter in accordance with the legal project plan. The project manager would be involved in the more administrative tasks around building the project plan and tracking progress. They will also be involved in gathering the information required on progress at legal team meetings. Unlike typical project management situations, the project manager role is more of an administrative role and is not to be seen as leading the meetings or driving the project. This will continue to be done by the senior lawyers involved on the legal matter.

The advantage of this type of model is that lawyers will continue to work in a manner similar to what they do today but with the project management capability injected by the project manager. Due to the non-legal skillset brought by the project manager, the cost of hiring one will be considerably lower than a mid-level associate. However, in the initial phase and largely due to the unknown value aspect by the law firm, the project manager's role will be viewed as an overhead cost. If the project manager's role proves to provide value to work matters and this is clearly demonstrated in the billings, planning, timing, and client satisfaction scores, then the law firm may in time begin to bill the project manager's time to the client. When this occurs, the project manager will then become part of the legal team and will facilitate the orchestration of activities and the resolution of issues in a timely and efficient manner. This will then leave the lawyers to focus on the legal issues at hand.

The disadvantage of this model is that in the early stages there may be some tension between the legal team and the project manager resulting in weaker project management capabilities overall. The legal team may not have the ability to raise issues related to scope changes and impacts to the project plan, nor will the project plan necessarily have the attention of the lawyer(s) leading the legal matter. Accordingly, the law firm may have skeptical teams working on legal matters and the law firm may experience some turnover on the side of the project manager's role. Only until the value of the project plan is recognized and the project manager is embraced for their responsibilities will the team be able to work and deliver the legal matter seamlessly. This model is expected to be a bigger change management initiative towards the adoption and acceptance and therefore will take longer to introduce, socialize, and get employees on-board.

Professional support lawyers

Projects managed with the help of a lawyer acting purely in a support capacity and not responsible for delivering the legal mandate

This model is similar to the model described just above with the difference that instead of a non-legal project manager, there is a lawyer assigned as the project manager. This is done by having a pool of legal project management professionals within the firm who are assigned to matters on an "as needed" basis. This group of legal professionals would typically be assigned to the larger matters with more financial risk either to the client or to the firm where a matter is being worked upon on a fixed fee basis. The group would have varying legal backgrounds so that they know about the area of the law and can fully appreciate the challenges to be faced by the legal team and also help with the substantive creation of achievable project plans.

The advantage of this model is that there is someone who understands the legal issues and would likely have a greater traction as a member of the team right from the start. In general project management theory, a project manager does not need to have a detailed knowledge of the specific streams of work they are managing, but it does help. By understanding, or as a lawyer with some knowledge in the area seen to have an understanding of the specific issues involved, the project manager in this model will have more say and driving power with the legal team to question estimates, ask questions to facilitate quicker issue resolution options, and drive the other lawyers to meet the appropriate budget.

A key disadvantage of this model is that there is not currently a plethora of lawyers that are also project managers. The market is changing and project management is being introduced to lawyers who are in the early stages of their career or in law schools. Hopefully, in 10 or so years' time this will not be an issue. However, many (if not the majority of) lawyers will not want to be "only" the project manager and will also want to be actively involved in the delivery of the substantive legal work. Therefore, this model can create some friction between the legal team responsible for delivery and the legal project managers who over-steps their boundaries. On a positive note, this model creates a different career path for lawyers and provides an opportunity for the legal world to create innovative roles where the goals of the lawyers and the skills of the project manager can be aligned.

In conclusion, all of these models have their strengths and weaknesses. Law firms will likely start with the simple model that fits into their existing firm culture and gradually move to another model (or a hybrid model) as they mature in capabilities and understand what works and does not work within their firm. Clients will also have an impact on the model that a law firm takes which coincidently is likely to be dependent on their own maturity. Clients experienced with the discipline of project management, such as engineering firms for example, will likely understand and support the inclusion of billable hours by the project manager who may or may not be a lawyer. Other clients will simply not deem it of any value to their legal work or see it as an administration function of the law firm and thus will not be willing to pay for time associated with delivering these services. Regardless of how the billing model is orchestrated, the law firm will need to factor the cost of the project management per se into the cost of delivering their work.

To remain profitable on fixed fee mandates and various other alternative fee arrangements, law firms will need to get a solid grasp on the full cost of delivery of the legal work and manage it properly. Much of the innovation in the law firm in terms of alternative fees will be fed by information that is delivered through the practice and discipline of project management.

Systematically tracking details of work as it is being done helps gather information to identify baselines on a diverse set of legal mandates. Having this information will help the law firm be able to effectively provide more innovative ways to price legal mandates with concrete historical pricing data and at the same time reduce risk associated with these alternative arrangements.

In the law firm of the future, legal project management will be the norm, just like the client dinner or the RFP process. Remember, not too long ago, RFPs were uncommon in law firms, but it is hard to get on a client's preferred vendor list without submitting one today. There will always be outliers and exceptions, but more often than not, that is exactly what they are – exceptions. Legal project management is here to stay and the law firms that accept this early on will simply have more time to get better at it.

A version of this article first appeared in The Future of Legal Services: Expert Analysis, *Second Edition, London: ARK Group, 2011*

Chapter 4:
The client value perspective

By Lann Wasson, associate director of legal project management at Husch Blackwell LLP

Understanding value from a client's perspective and thinking strategically about how one can partner with clients has become more vital to service delivery. In recent years the emphasis clients have placed on value has grown considerably. For instance, in 2015 the Wicker Park Group reviewed 800 of its client interviews from 2011–2014 and observed that, "the percentage of clients talking about the importance of value increased from 43 percent in 2011 to an astounding 73 percent in 2014."[1] The Chicago based consultancy reached this conclusion, "Clearly value is becoming vastly more important as a differentiator. As law firms continue to invest in client service, it is more important than ever that they define value from a client's point of view down to each individual person." During this same period, the Association of Corporate Counsel (ACC) recognized that in-house counsel faced a similar challenge from their own internal clients. In its 2011 Value Challenge Guide to Project Management, the ACC noted "the overarching challenge is the need to define and articulate the department's value in business terms, to the CEO, CFO, and other executive management."[2] One of the ways law firms and law departments alike have responded to demands for greater value is through the adoption of Legal Project Management (LPM) techniques, such as scoping and budgeting which take into account the business context of the legal issue. The best lawyers have also taken steps to align their priorities and resources more closely with clients and put in place metrics and scorecards to measure performance, often with the aid of legal project management and operations professionals.

Yet, based on the results of industry surveys, on the whole there remains a substantial gap in the perception of value delivered and value received in the industry as a whole. Over the last five years Altman Weil, Hildebrandt Baker Robins, and others have assessed the degree to which law firms have demonstrated their understanding of client business objectives and expectations. The low ranks and disparity between the ratings of chief legal officers and their law firm counterparts tells a sobering story. When asked to provide an example of a time when lawyers exceeded expectations, one in-house advocate of LPM even described the scenario as the "Yeti" of legal work. From the law department standpoint, the BTI Consulting Group reported that not only has there been an increasing turnover of general counsel over the last six years, but that companies have charged their new Chief Legal Officers with adding value and supporting the organization.[3] Many law departments are tackling those mandates by implementing rigorous project management programs and by aligning in-house counsel with their business units.

Why are opportunities missed?

While it's quite common to short list the obstacles to delivering higher value, the sheer number of reasons why misalignment occurs underscores the need to pay attention to each client's particular situation. In certain circumstances, the business priorities of the law department may be focused elsewhere in response to restructuring or M&A activity, or were more intensely focused in some areas but not others. The background and tenure of the General Counsel also influences where change begins and how much pressure is applied. Many clients have missed opportunities to clarify higher level expectations in their Outside Counsel Guidelines, despite a concentration on billing procedures. In other instances, law departments are just starting or still in the process of implementing scorecards and e-billing technology and likely require a number of years of performance data before acting on the results. And, it's often the case when law departments are ready to align spend with performance, they simply don't engage in these conversations. Instead, they turn off the faucet and shift work elsewhere, based on the assumption that if a law firm hasn't brought their practice wisdom to the table by this point, they just don't get it. Finally, based on the findings in "Unless You Ask",[4] the ACC's 2016 guide to increase urgency and drive change, there is simply reluctance on the part of some inside counsel to demand greater change.

In private practice the reflection of this sentiment is summed up by the expression, "the client hasn't asked for it." While it's true that some lawyers simply resist change, underlying this statement is often a desire to be more prepared for these types of conversations. After all, law firms have spent decades coaching their partners on how to cross-sell, since compensation systems focus on revenue and reward time spent on a matter instead of value conferred. It's a much more recent exercise to host a meeting where one asks broad, open ended questions about the organization, objectives, and priorities and then listens carefully to concerns, pain points, and other challenges. Many lawyers, who by training tend to dive immediately into the details, find it challenging to keep the conversation near the top of the funnel. Communicating the outcomes of the dialogue to the entire client team also requires partners to move beyond the Hub and Spoke model which has traditionally dominated client interactions. Finally, these conversations tend to include an analysis of data, sometimes implicit descriptions of process design and references to large scale technology systems, which many lawyers are much less familiar with and comfortable speaking about.

While many of these obstacles will undoubtedly take time to resolve and some may prove to be intractable, there are still a number of techniques innovative partners and their colleagues inside law departments can use to start pushing the flywheel forward. It's important to remember that since McKinsey introduced the 7S Framework in the late 1970s, the value of alignment has been a central management theme in creating effective organizations. Today, when leading scholars from Robert Kaplan and David Norton to Jim Collins study the performance of Hall of Fame companies, they underscore the enormous benefits alignment provides people at all levels of a company, as well as the rest of the supply chain. Fred Gluck, founder of McKinsey's Strategy Practice and former managing director of the firm, has observed that when professionals synthesize all of the data, industry trends, and conversations of strategic planning into a few "strategic rules of thumb," stakeholders can use that clarity to drive innovation and value.[5]

The four "rules of thumb"

One way to distill some of these "strategic rules of thumb" is by looking at the characteristics which distinguished the ACC Value Champions from the rest of the industry over the last four years. Established in 2012, the Value Champion program recognizes the achievements of law departments driving value in three areas: spending, predictability, and outcomes. The Value Champion initiatives indicate that there are four primary attributes that lead to successful outcomes:

- Value conversations must be a collaborative undertaking;
- Value conversations are focused on creative business solutions instead of narrow legal issues;
- Participants should come from diverse backgrounds; and
- The language and techniques used to communicate value are grounded in the operational practices of each company.

While each Value Champion program shares these common attributes, it's equally important to remember that these characteristics coalesced in unique ways during each initiative.

The fundamental difference in the Value Champion programs is that sponsors did not hold conversations about alignment in a vacuum. Examples from the Value Champions show how these law departments took a more inclusive approach. After engaging their procurement team, Aon's Peter Lieb and Audrey Rubin offered this advice to other companies interested in value initiatives. "It's key to listen to what the business needs and align to its priorities and goals" (2016 Value Champions).[6] Farrah Pepper from General Electric concurs. "At GE, value speaks for itself. We sat down with people to discover their pain points, and designed our program to address them. Once people try it, they keep coming back" (2016 Value Champions). The ACC describes the approach that Terena Rodrigues from Embraer used. "The first step was to define, in consultation with their clients, critical items in the performance of the legal department. These requirements – quality, timeliness and flexibility – became the premises to define the Key Performance Indicators on which products and services would be evaluated" (2014 Value Champions).[7] Finally, Ellen Pekilis from the CSA Group even took the conversation a step further. The ACC reported, "Through a series of monthly half-day meetings, Pekilis and her staff went through the corporate business plan line by line, identifying the legal work necessary to enable each line item in the plan, then grouping tasks by theme or type of legal skill required" (2014 Value Championship). What each of these initiatives demonstrates is that a joint conversation that crosses the links in the value chain was crucial for alignment.

All too often when client teams strategize about opportunities to provide more value, in-house counsel are absent from the meeting. Pam Woldow, as a partner at the global legal consulting firm Edge International, recognized the benefits of bringing inside counsel into the conversation when she said, "In our LPM training, we see better results when we focus more on client teams...We have seen even greater and more immediate benefits when we include lawyers from the client side in training – not just to watch, but to build their needs, structure and internal procedures into the fabric of the training."[8] The Wicker Park Group concurs, "The only way to successfully accomplish that [defining value] is to engage the client in ongoing, meaningful conversation on the topic and never assume that last year's definition of value is the same as the current definition."[9] Partners should emulate their colleagues inside law departments and start bridging the gap by bringing both internal and external stakeholders together.

The second rule of thumb is to keep these conversations focused on achieving business solutions instead of resolving a more narrow legal issue. Sometimes, it is even necessary to take a step back and clarify what success looks like. One example that Husch Blackwell uses in its LPM workshops comes from David Cambria, the Global Director of Operations for the Law Department of Archer Daniels Midland (ADM), who spoke a few years ago about how one law firm exceeded ADM's expectations. In response to an RFP, this firm provided a continuum of outcomes based on their practice wisdom and experience, which the ADM team then reviewed with their business unit. From there, ADM was able to come up with a plan of attack that included some business actions in the marketplace as well as a legal strategy. From David Cambria's perspective, the law firm succeeded because they didn't assume they knew how to get to the end and instead worked collaboratively with ADM to clarify success and get to a broader, more creative solution. In the end, it was a good outcome for ADM because of the alignment up and down the value chain.

The experience of the Value Champions reflects the same business focused and solution based approach. In her 2014 initiative, Kathleen O'Connor from JP Morgan Chase & Company mentioned that her team attempted to, "resolve matters using business solutions where possible," so that a customer's problem didn't become a legal issue (2014 Value Champions). She continued, "our team is customer focused; we're trying to find resolutions. This is not a sea change, but it was an opportunity to partner closely with our business clients" (2014 Value Champions). During his 2016 Value Champion initiative, Michael Kaplan from Red Robin described his team's approach this way, "Increasingly legal departments like ours are looking to legal providers for solutions to broader business problems, taking more of a product and implementation approach rather than simply providing legal advice on individual matters" (2016 Value Champions). By engaging stakeholders in a conversation focused on the success of the business instead of simply the legal issues, lawyers both in private practice and in-house can develop broader, more creative business solutions.

The third characteristic of the Value Champion programs was the composition of the teams brought in to work on the problem. To improve their overall capabilities, many of these law departments included people at the table with a variety of skillsets from other areas of the business. Likewise some in-house counsel reached out to their law firms for non-legal expertise to improve cross-functional collaboration. For AIG's 2015 project, the ACC reported, "They focused on two key elements: building a multidisciplinary team with diverse areas of expertise, and designing scalable processes and technology... The Process & Information Excellence team helps the legal department understand legal spend and outcomes and make better decisions" (2015 Value Champions).[10] In 2016 Rick Musgrave from Husky Injection Molding Systems described their approach this way. "The tools were created totally in-house by cross-functional teams with representatives from engineering, marketing, and the executive level; the legal team 'quarterbacked the development and implementation of these tools'" (2016 Value Champions). In our experience working directly with law departments, clients have found it invaluable when partners bring their cross-functional expertise, process design, and technology acumen to the table.

The fourth rule of thumb in value conversations is to listen for and incorporate the language and techniques of the operational side of the company in the solution. In its 2014 Value Champion report, the ACC noted that, "As legal departments align more closely with their customers and apply strategies and tactics common to the business units they serve; they are shifting their culture to one of greater transparency, solid partnerships and more sophisticated practice" (2014 Value Champions). Becoming more operationally aware is central to effective communication and adoption, but it also may be critical to innovation. In September 2016, Dr. Clayton Christensen introduced a concept called "the job to be done" which complements his theory of disruption in the "Innovator's Dilemma". In a nutshell, Christensen observed that knowing more about one's customers doesn't predict the success of an innovation. "What they really need to home in on is the progress that the customer is trying to make in a given circumstance-what the customer hopes to accomplish."[11] This insight allows companies to differentiate their offering in ways competitors aren't likely to copy or even comprehend. In the context of the legal industry, firms that understand "the job to be done" can more effectively engage in-house counsel and their business operations and provide greater value in ways that other firms simply can't emulate.

Three examples from the Value Champions demonstrate just how central operational awareness was for achieving a successful outcome. In his 2014 initiative at Caterpillar, Inc., Byron Buck mentioned how his team incorporated the lane strategies used in manufacturing operations into their approach. "We started drawing connections that could apply to the legal department. A logical outgrowth of that strategy was that legal documents span a spectrum from standard to highly customized." He concluded, "How you work is as important as what your work produces. For us, change management and project management were key, as well as buy-in and commitment from the company's senior leadership" (2014 Value Champions). When Chris Smith outlined the important elements of his 2014 initiative at Hyundai Motor Manufacturing Alabama, LLC, he said "it's important to understand the corporate culture in which the legal department was working. Manufacturing concepts are essential to understanding our internal customers, who look for results in numbers rather than words" (2014 Value Champions). Finally, in 2015 SSM Health's Patti Williams related that, "Managing relationships with business leaders was a primary focus from the start... By quickly becoming more involved and engaged in operational issues, team members became more attuned to the specific needs of those business leaders" (2015 Value Champions). By including clients and a broader team of stakeholders and focusing on business solutions and the operational dynamics unique to each business unit, these champions successfully linked their objectives together and drove value through their business and supply chain.

Applying the four principles

With these four rules of thumb from the Value Champions in mind, let's consider a few areas where law firms and law departments can work together to apply these principles to value conversations. One of the core principles of legal project management is to keep all stakeholders in the loop all of the time. When law departments do outline value concretely in their Outside Counsel Guidelines, legal project management professionals should summarize and communicate these objectives to the broader client team. Sometimes, these guidelines also offer operational clues on how a client and their business units communicate. For instance, guidelines from one of the Value Champions stand out because it includes a process map. Knowing that this was an important mode of communication, Husch Blackwell's team utilized the same approach and tools when responding to the law department's RFP. In fact, during one meeting last year a member of the client's team actually stopped the meeting to express their gratitude for paying attention to their communication preferences. In other conversations, if one is tuned to listening for the steps of a workflow, one might hear the thoughtfulness of in-house counsel in formulating their processes. In our experience, drawing out the workflow steps in TaskMap can aid a law department as they develop their process further.

At a higher level, law firms have opportunities to clarify their understanding of law department goals and objectives as well as aid in-house counsel in their own efforts at strategic planning and alignment with their internal clients. Of the tools used to communicate strategy and the processes and systems used to implement it, strategy maps can be very effective in concisely describing the drivers of value and how initiatives align with department objectives. Over a decade ago, Robert Kaplan and David Norton introduced strategy maps as a practical means to engage employee's with their company's balanced scorecard. The challenge today is to simplify the format so the visual design focuses on the priorities and programs relevant to the law department. To that end, Husch Blackwell's LPM team distilled and consolidated observations and insights from client initiatives, industry conferences, and other conversations into a benchmark law department strategy map. Depending on the purpose of the meeting, the team may share the benchmark map, design a customized map based on the client's portrayal of their objectives and tactics and even offer to revise the custom map based on their subsequent feedback. Within the law firm, these maps can also be a tremendous tool to share the client's value perspective with the broader legal team. On the whole, finding more structured ways of bringing cross-functional insights to bear on value conversations creates opportunities for partners and in-house counsel to work collaboratively in ways that benefit the whole value chain.

The last area where law firms and in-house counsel can work together to drive value regards collaboration around metrics and scorecards. Usually, the challenge for law firms is to encourage partners to ask clients how they evaluate law firm performance on matters and to share these ratings on a regular basis with their team. However, even when attorneys pursue this kind of feedback, their own performance is measured by altogether different criteria in end-of-year reviews. One of the insights from Gallup's work on employee engagement is that you can't measure and manage employee and customer experiences as separate entities. You must measure them in tandem. Gallup illustrates this idea using the measurement of blood pressure as the indicator of how well the circulatory (employee) and respiratory (customer) systems are working together.[12] Measuring alignment with objectives and expectations is like measuring vital signs. Aligning client metrics and scorecards with partner and team performance reviews not only takes the pulse of the relationship but also reality tests the aspirations of partners and the outlook for future engagements.

The importance of delivering greater value in client engagements cannot be understated. Despite the institutional challenges within law firms, innovative partners have a number of legal project management techniques at their disposal to align their teams more closely with law department goals and objectives. The four strategic rules of thumb, derived from the practices Value Champions used to achieve their objectives, can guide partners as they engage in-house counsel in value conversations. Client teams that include in-house stakeholders in planning, focus on creative business solutions, bring cross-functional resources and expertise to the table, and pay attention to operational communications are more likely to create a broader based alignment with client goals and objectives. When applied like concrete actions, such as developing process and strategy maps and encouraging alignment around performance metrics, these actions can deliver greater value throughout the entire value chain.

References

1. Wicker Park Group, "How Do Your Clients Define Value," May 26, 2015. See: http://wickerparkgroup.com/2015/05/26/how-do-your-clients-define-value/
2. Association of Corporate Counsel, "ACC Value Challenge: Guide to Project Management", October 11, 2011. See:http://www.acc.com/advocacy/valuechallenge/toolkit/loader.cfm?csModule=security/getfile&pageid=1293786&recorded=1
3. Kurt Orzeck "General Counsel Turnover Highest In 13 Years," February 20, 2014. See: https://www.law360.com/articles/511849/general-counsel-turnover-highest-in-13-years
4. D. Casey Flaherty with Association of Corporate Counsel, "Unless You Ask: A Guide for Law Departments To Get More From External Relationships," June 14, 2016. See: http://www.acc.com/vl/public/Article/loader.cfm?csModule=security/getfile&pageid=1432511&page=/valuechallenge/index.cfm&qstring=&title=Unless%20You%20Ask%3A%20A%20Guide%20For%20Law%20Departments%20to%20Get%20More%20From%20External%20Relationships&recorded=1

5. Fred Gluck, Michael G. Jacobides, and Dan Simpson, "Synthesis, capabilities, and overlooked insights: Next frontiers for strategists, September 2014. See: http://www.mckinsey.com/business-functions/strategy-and-corporate-finance/our-insights/synthesis-capabilities-and-overlooked-insights
6. Association of Corporate Counsel, "2016 Value Champions," September 2016. See: http://www.accvaluechallenge-digital.com/accvaluechallenge/valuechampion201609?pg=1#pg1
7. Association of Corporate Counsel, "2014 Value Champions," September 2014. See: http://www.accvaluechallenge-digital.com/accvaluechallenge/value_champions_supplement_sept_2014?pg=1#pg1
8. Pam Woldow and Doug Richardson, "A New Approach to Collaboration: Legal Project Management", August 16, 2011. See: http://www.pamwoldow.com/2011/08/16/a-new-approach-to-collaboration-legal-project-management/
9. See note 1.
10. Association of Corporate Counsel, "2015 Value Champions," September 2015. See: http://www.accvaluechallenge-digital.com/accvaluechallenge/2015valuechampions?pg=1#pg1
11. Christensen C., Hall T., Dillon T., and Duncan D., S., "Know Your Customers' 'Jobs to be Done'", Harvard Business Review, September 2016.
12. John H. Fleming and Jim Asplund, Human Sigma, New York: Gallup Press, 2007.

Chapter 5:
E-discovery and legal project management

By Zena Applebaum, director of competitive intelligence at Bennett Jones LLP

Business intelligence (BI), or knowing what a firm knows, is not activity for activity's sake. Instead the goal of BI, in whatever form and with whichever inputs, should be geared towards helping firms deliver a more efficient service to clients and thereby reduce their bottom line or increase profitability.

There are two trends in law firms today that are linked to the BI process. The first, e-discovery, creates data almost by accident and the second, legal project management (LPM), takes all of the data floating around in firms and turns them into a client-driven project plan. The two trends are very different, but both involve looking at documents, data, and the creation of processes for storing, capturing, and using intelligence.

E-discovery/document management

Written by Mark Gediman, director of information serives at Best Best & Krieger LLP

What is e-discovery?

Just saying the term "e-discovery" to your information technology director will cause him or her to grab for the antacids, as the advent of e-discovery has fundamentally changed the way in which firms treat and store electronic information. Firms have had to adapt their technology to make finding internal information easier, as well as making sure that when information is deleted it cannot be reconstructed. Consequently, new tools and resources have been developed to assist the firm when responding to e-discovery requests. Their onerous requirements have become the BI practitioner's treasure trove.

Before looking at the BI applications, a good definition of e-discovery and its parts and pieces will be helpful. E-discovery is short for the phrase "electronic discovery" and applies to the exchange of electronically stored information among litigants during the course of civil litigation.[1] When the US Federal Rules of Civil Procedure were amended in 2006, it provided a comprehensive approach to handling this type of information.[2]

The types of electronic information covered by e-discovery include (but are not limited to) "word processing documents, e-mail messages, electronic spreadsheets, different image or sound files, and material from databases".[3] Since these are documents produced by the firm, managing them is usually part of the firm's overall risk management strategy. The result is that firms typically invest in the latest tools and technologies for managing the storage and retrieval of these important records.

Changed inner workings

E-discovery requirements have prompted the creation of search and retrieval tools that make the retrieval of relevant data files much easier and more cost-effective. When coupled with the firm's record management system, the firm is able to impose document retention requirements across data repositories while at the same time keeping them organized and accessible.

Preservation of metadata is another important component of a successful e-discovery process. Metadata is defined as "structured information that describes, explains, locates, and otherwise makes it easier to retrieve and use an information resource".[4] Put simply, metadata contains information about who created a document, who edited it, who viewed it, when it was created and edited, what application was used to create it, and much, much more. Metadata is the data that is tacitly created as a by-product of the actual document.

A good overview of the functions that a firm should implement to address the requirements of e-discovery is given in Figure 1.

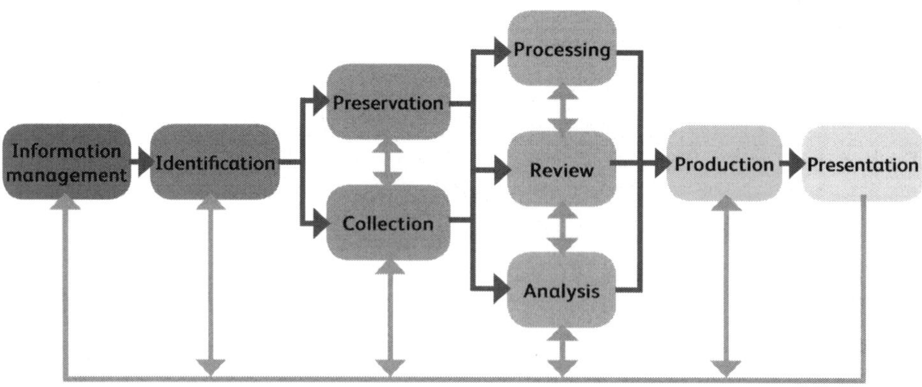

Figure 1: Electronic discovery reference model

The systems currently used by firms have to do more than just store and profile documents. These systems have to allow for the preservation, collection, review, analysis, and production of information without affecting the underlying document and its metadata in any way. As can be seen from Figure 1, these requirements should be integral to any document management process. One can also begin to see how the data inputs available for BI analysis from the e-discovery process are dense and rich.

As a result, document management repositories now more closely resemble the structure found in the physical files. Document management systems (DMSs) now offer a matter-centric structure with different document types stored in specific folders. If one has Client XYZ Company with a billing number of 11111, each matter opened on behalf of the client would have its own location in the DMS. These locations are sometimes called worksites and make it easier to organize the documents produced for that matter. Under this scheme, the trademark management matter would have its own unique storage area in a structure similar to that found in the physical file. Any lawyer billing Client XYZ in the same matter would file all the documents together under the same matter number. Therefore it can begin to be assessed, from a BI perspective, which lawyers work together on which types of files, etc., or what types of matters are or are not handled for a certain client.

The e-discovery toolbox

There are many tools currently on the market to assist with finding information in response to an e-discovery request. These range from global network search products such as Discovery Accelerator, Enterprise Vault, and Applied Discovery to products specifically developed to handle documents produced as part of a response to an e-discovery request, such as Concordance and LiveNote.

Global search tools are especially helpful when the firm has recently instigated a document filing policy or has incomplete compliance with this policy. In either of these circumstances, every data set must be searched to comply with the e-discovery request. Since document locations are not restricted to the appropriate client/matter worksite, it is necessary to use a tool that can search across different data types and platforms. Most tools of this type also allow the item to be viewed without affecting its metadata and allow its chain of custody to be seen. These are very important considerations when responding to an e-discovery request. The key to these applications is to index, filter, and compile both the data and the metadata without affecting either one.

E-discovery inputs for business intelligence

With this basic understanding of e-discovery and its processes, how these resources can be applied to the gathering of BI can be considered. The organization of the firm's data imposed by the requirements of e-discovery has made mining this data not just possible but also much easier than in the past. When these tools are added into the mix, the amount of information that is accessible to users increases.

Part of the BI process involves taking the material found during the course of research and organizing it to see whether trends or other common factors emerge. Products such as Law PreDiscovery allow the researcher to include images of physical documents along with classification information in these search results. Then one should use products such as Concordance to put all of the information together where it can be assimilated and analyzed for best effect.

Software tools such as Discovery Accelerator make it much easier to find documents on the network that have not been filed in the appropriate client matter worksites. Items from such disparate databases as e-mail or the shared network become readily available when using these tools. Software tools also allow certain documents to be preserved without changing the metadata, which allows the researcher to use the metadata as a resource.

There are other tools that have some "off label" uses for BI. In other words, these tools are created for an entirely different purpose but can be readily adapted and appropriated for BI. Most firms have tools to assist them in retrieving information from their internal databases. These can include case analysis software, DMS search engines, financial analytic software, e-mail search tools, OCR software, and even billing software.

Using case analysis software in an off-label approach can indicate which published opinions have become the main precedents in their field. There can be value in being able to show that legal arguments made by the firm or an opposing firm have strongly influenced areas of law, not to mention the attorneys who made those arguments. The marketing value of knowing what one knows in this case could be hugely beneficial.

There is a treasure trove of information in the firm's documents. Most firms use a search engine to make it easier to find documents on a particular topic or a specific document from the material stored in the DMS. DMS search engines such as Recommind or Lexis Search Advantage make it possible to precisely set the search criteria to retrieve a targeted search result. There are several types of information that this search capability makes simpler to get which will support firm growth and development. From pleadings to e-mail, correspondence to contracts, the DMS can be a wealth of information to the BI researcher.

Here is a quick look at the actual value some representative documents can have for BI:

- **Litigation documents** encountered or created by the firm in the course of litigation can provide a wealth of information, including contact information and intelligence on business practices and may even have rate information in the form of a fee request. If a firm digitizes court-related documents from all parties and stores them in the DMS, it would have full access to the information mentioned above.
- **Correspondence** can contain a wide variety of information. This can range from the mundane details of a client's restaurant preference to the strategic details of how to conduct a negotiation with a rival firm.
- **E-mail** can answer some questions including: Who does a great job responding to requests for proposals? Who is good at talking to the press? Are there internal groups that are great at sharing information?
- **Contracts:** Are there contracts for clients that can be used by the firm? And how about touting the firm's expertise in a particular area using the firm's best practice documents as industry standards?
- **Finding subject matter specialists:** Every firm has attorneys who have a large amount of experience in a specific subject or area of law. Most people send out firm-wide e-mails that have "Does anyone have experience…" in the subject line, which are usually ignored. This is not to be despaired over, as by running a search on the topic in the DMS and ranking it by author in descending order instantly produces a list of the people in the firm that are the experts in that area. Not only does this produce a name, but when sending an e-mail a connection can be made by making a personalized plea for assistance.

- **Legal service/fee agreements:** Retrieving these agreements based on a common service or client type can provide the vehicle for a survey of different terms and language. Coupled with the information obtained from the billing system, this produces the information needed for an in-depth analysis of the firm's client relationships.
- **Knowledge management (KM) tools** make it easier to group documents and find them. More on this can be found in Chapter 5.

The requirements placed upon firms following the advent of e-discovery have created a treasure trove of data for the BI researcher. The tools that have been developed in response to these requirements have made it easier for the researcher to find and organize the data. E-discovery has made BI research simple.

Legal project management

LPM was largely developed in relation to client requests rather than a change in policy (as was the case with e-discovery), following the client push for price certainty in engagements, and the need for clients to manage their external counsel budgets.

Clients began to force law firms into estimating the cost of a particular legal matter and then to more or less stick to that estimate. While new for law firms, the practice of estimation has long been used in so many other professions, from trades to software implementation. In some industries, such as the construction industry, delays and extraneous costs are often passed back to the contractor. Law firms are not yet at that stage. LPM is a step in that direction. It is a plan or contract that lays out the process a firm suggests for a particular mandate or set of mandates provided to the client about how much, how long, and how involved a project will be.

How it works

Borrowing and building on established business processes such as Six Sigma and the International Organization for Standardization regulations, LPM encompasses accurate budget forecasts, deliverable work plans and flexible, customizable, real-time financial reporting systems. Measuring client budget and work plan performance on a quarterly, monthly, weekly – or even daily – basis, can enable the strategic, data-driven decisions that lead to optimal outcomes.

Questions that should arise from the LPM process include:

- What are a client's goals in successfully resolving the matter?
- Where has the client identified risk or where has the law firm indicated there may be risk?
- Does the client have particular pricing parameters or pricing arrangements in mind?
- How does the client want its work to be managed?

The answers to such questions provide the framework for the project plan. Answering these questions will not only help those involved in the LPM devise a plan for the matter, but it will also assure the client of the firm's commitment to client service.

Once the questions are answered, the firm can then begin the process (if it has not done so already in anticipation of the answers) of pulling out the appropriate BI inputs or historic data to determine the best ways to meet the client's staffing, budget, scheduling, and billing needs to facilitate the matter in a way that is acceptable to the client and the firm.

Communication

Aside from key supporting BI, one of the keys to the success of a well implemented LPM matter is open and frank communication with clients throughout the engagement. Some firms work on a "relationship partner" model, where one partner is responsible for reporting back to clients at weekly, monthly, or other intervals about the progress of the mandate. As with other areas of law firm management, there are also technological or LPM reporting tools that firms can use to update clients and lawyers alike on the time and expense of each item and tasks that still remain to be completed with deadlines and milestone dates.

Knowledge management and legal process management

If KM deals with the practice of law, the LMP deals with the business of law. That is to say that KM is focused on making the practice of law quicker and more efficient for clients whereas LMP improves the process and business outcomes for law firms. Table 1 lists some of the differences between KM and LPM.[5]

	Knowledge management	Legal project management
Professional proficiency required	Requires professional expertise	Indifferent to professional expertise
Efficiency promoted	Promotes more efficient performance of tasks	Promotes more efficient assignment and resasignment of tasks
Methodology focus	Focuses on the practice of law	Focused on the processes of legal practice
Capital maximized	Maximizes the use of intellectual property resources	Maximizes the use of human resources
Benefit realized	Subject matter improvement	Process improvement
Human capital impact	Better informed resources	Better utilized resources
Price and deadlines	Unpredictable	Manages predictability

Table 1: A comparison of knowledge management and legal project management

Notwithstanding the differences, both KM and LPM can improve access to expertise and resources while improving efficiencies and increasing profitability. Taken together, the results of a combined effort would be the underpinnings of a world-class law firm BI – or know what one knows – program. Each can stand on its own as a harbinger of change within firms.

Firms applying legal practice management

There are many firms in North America and elsewhere that have implemented successful LPM programs over the past few years. In 2009, Dechert LLP[6] was one of the first law firms in the US to establish a firm-wide project management department. At Dechert, project planning is

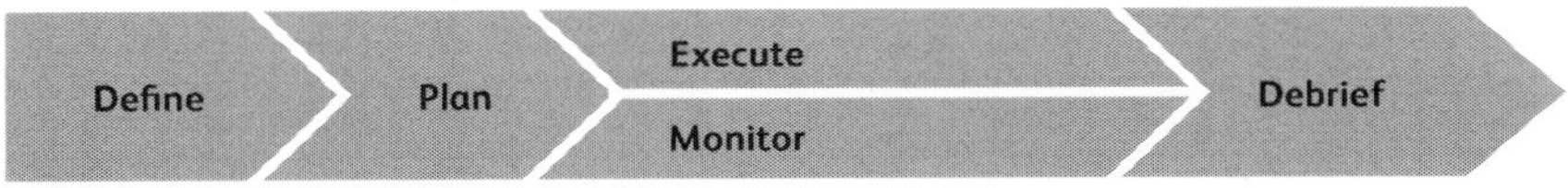

Figure 2: A four-phase project management plan

the first step in any engagement. The firm collaborates with clients to identify key business objectives and makes strategic decisions that are unique for each matter.

In 2011, Crowell & Moring[7] initiated a firm-wide rollout of LPM as an extension of its value-based billing approach to client matters. Nixon Peabody[8] has also implemented a project management program that is best described by the firm in four phases shown in Figure 2. Canadian firm McCarthy Tétrault[9] has implemented a trademarked legal process management program called Dialogue Project Management® to increase predictability and control costs. The Dialogue Project Management® system is based on the general principles of the Project Management Institute and is supported by proprietary tools and techniques developed for use by the firm's lawyers.

The firms listed are not exhaustive but the examples are designed to demonstrate the breadth of service offerings, as well the different approaches to marketing LPM, and are underscored by the various BI inputs. Chapter 11 provides an in-depth case study of how to create and market LPM in a firm, courtesy of Seyfath Shaw.

E-discovery and legal project management as data

It can be seen how e-discovery, legal billing rates, and other inputs combine in LPM, which only scratches the surface of the potential power "big data" has in the legal industry. Many other sources of data can be analyzed to offer insights and identify trends. Service of process records can help legal professionals identify litigation trends; trademark filings can support intellectual property practitioners' efforts to gain competitive advantage; and commercial lending activity can help mergers and acquisitions counsel better predict risk. What is more, as noted above firms are marketing these capabilities to clients to demonstrate their commitment to efficiency and client engagement. BI is not just a winning formula for firms; it represents a win for clients as well.

A version of this article first appeared in Applebaum, Z. Business Intelligence for Law Firms, *London: ARK Group, 2011*

References

1. Scheindlin, S.A., Moore's Federal Practice, *E-Discovery: The Newly Amended Federal Rules of Civil Procedure*, Part I., Background – The Need for the New Rules, Matthew Bender, 2006.
2. Ibid.
3. Ibid. Amendment to Rule 37.
4. National Information Standards Organization, *Understanding Metadata*, NISO Press, United States, 2006. Available at: http://www.niso.org/publications/press/UnderstandingMetadata.pdf, accessed September 19, 2012.
5. Bridgesmith, L. ERM Legal Solutions LLC 'Wisdom and choreography: How KM and LPM help create the legal dance.' In: *Project Management: the Perfect Juggling Act*, ILTA White Paper, September 2012.
6. www.dechert.com, accessed September 19, 2012.
7. http://www.crowell.com/about/innovation-in-service/legal-project-management, accessed September 19, 2012.
8. http://www.nixonpeabody.com/legal_project_ management, accessed September 19, 2012.
9. http://www.mccarthy.ca/Project_Management.aspx, accessed September 19, 2012.

Chapter 6:
Creating valuable knowledge in the firm through legal project management

By Lann Wasson, associate director of legal project management at Husch Blackwell LLP

Demand remains flat. Margins remain thin. Partner profits are stagnant. Large law firm leaders overwhelmingly acknowledge these trends, according to the latest surveys by Altman Weil, Thomson Reuters, and City/Hildebrandt. Yet, few firms have proactively adopted approaches like legal project management and process re-engineering that really challenge the way lawyers work to improve service delivery and their bottom line. To protect short term growth and productivity, most firms have instead focused on controlling direct and indirect expenses, closely managing equity status and associate hiring, and some have even outsourced administrative functions to lower cost regions.

As clients become more adept at comparing the performance of their panel counsel, law firms that find ways to provide more value at a lower cost of production will have an advantage over firms which simply try to keep pace with the competition. The 2017 Citi/Hildebrandt Client Advisory notes "in a market where clients want the most efficient delivery of legal services, the market will reward law firms who focus on operational efficiency in its broadest sense — not just managing expenses, but transforming the way they run their firms and deliver legal services."[1] Furthermore, both the 2017 Report on the State of the Legal Market by the Georgetown Law Center and Thomson Reuters[2] and the 2016 Law Firms in Transition report by Altman Weil[3] cite evidence that suggests that a proactive posture towards improving the delivery of legal services enables firms to reap more financial benefits as their programs mature.

As a systematic approach to scoping, planning, and managing legal work within agreed upon time, budget, and performance requirements, Legal Project Management (LPM) is one of the best approaches firms can use to address these challenges. As a standalone program, project management succeeds because scoping aligns law firm tactics with law department objectives, brings the business context of the matter into focus, and reduces the chance that unwanted work will be done in the first place. Managing towards a budget often results in less scope creep and write offs, greater attention paid to staffing and leverage, and ultimately higher realization and profitability. Likewise, a stronger emphasis on timely communication prevents surprises that tend to sour relationships. Much like other belt-tightening efforts to manage expenses at the firm level, legal project management provides a framework to trim away the fat at the matter level.

What's missing in many LPM initiatives is that legal project management also has the potential to coordinate an even wider range of activities from the domains of knowledge management, business analysis, and technology that can transform service delivery beyond what project management alone can achieve. While a thorough discussion of all of these areas is beyond the scope of this paper, the benefits of a more coordinated approach are evident by looking at how project management can lay a foundation for process improvement and how a greater emphasis on process knowledge can enhance the value of LPM activities.

Launching the legal project management program

For those firms thinking strategically about improving service delivery, the best starting point is often a Legal Project Management program because it sets in motion the standardization of legal work by introducing a framework that lawyers follow throughout the matter lifecycle. For the purpose of this discussion, project management refers generally to the approach found in the Project Management Institute's (PMI) Body of Knowledge. As a more structured approach to service delivery, legal project management directly responds to client demands for predictability, transparency, and cost-effectiveness by providing the techniques and training to define, communicate, and manage matters to the scope, budget, and schedule. Unlike the way project management is used in industries such as construction and software development, legal project management is often based on a simplified framework and playbook that allows attorneys to continue to adapt to the unique characteristics and often adversarial dynamics of their work.

Process improvement initiatives on the other hand frequently begin at a practice level and are often very specific to a type of legal work, which makes the process more difficult to replicate across the firm as a whole. During my education in Lean Six Sigma, the notion that standard work was a prerequisite for improvement was underscored by a former GE

Master Black Belt trainer who advised us that improvement measures would fail if a company lacked a commitment to standard work. Even though lawyers at Husch Blackwell had experienced some early success in refining M&A processes, the firm made the strategic decision that project management was the one process which could have the most impact in every area of the firm. The fruits of this decision are evident today as scoping statements and budget templates propagate throughout the firm as lawyers share their success stories with their colleagues in other offices and practices.

During the first wave of large law firm initiatives, the mere existence of a legal project management program was seen as a differentiator, just as the presence of a pricing professional was considered responsive to client needs. However, many of these early programs focused almost exclusively on training and lacked the standards necessary to sustain a substantive offering. To be sure, practicing any of the components of legal project management is worthwhile – and lawyers should adjust the level of detail to fit the engagement. The challenge is to create a systematic approach that takes advantage of the synergy among LPM activities, instead of offering partners a buffet of tools and techniques. Clients and law firms alike are not well served when there are as many flavors of project management as there are partners in the firm. Clients too are savvier now about the substance of these programs and insist that lawyers who pitch project management actually practice project management.

At Husch Blackwell, the director of legal project management and strategic pricing recognized this pitfall early on. To counter this tendency among partners, the director created a task force with representation from all levels of the firm, including paralegals, associates, a director of operations, a practice group chair, and management committee member. The task force met over a period of months to openly discuss and refine project management standards. Then the director vetted the standards at the highest levels of firm leadership to secure its adoption as the firm's standard and the practical extension of the firm's strategic initiative. Finally, at leadership meetings executives reinforced the need for partners to abide by program standards in order to fulfill the firm's brand promise.

Central to all of the standards in Husch Blackwell's program is the statement that each standard should be performed whether the client has asked for it or not. The firm's LPM training workshops also emphasize the importance of being proactive since it takes a concerted investment of one's time and reflection on one's experience to perform these tasks well. Recent research published by Thomson Reuters and Altman Weil confirms that law firms which use greater rigor to understand and manage these techniques outperform and are more profitable than firms which merely react under client pressure. Husch Blackwell's experience bears this out. A forward looking, standards based approach results in better client service and financial performance on matters managed under the guidelines of the program.

Some law departments are also focused on developing project management standards and even collaborate within industry associations, such as the ABA's Task Force on legal project management and the Corporate Legal Operations Consortium (CLOC).

Engaging a law department in a discussion about the benefits and challenges of legal project management is a prime opportunity to listen to what a client values and learn more about the business context of the firm's matters. Indeed, scoping done well provides all the stakeholders with an understanding of what successful outcomes look like and the priorities of the business organization. It even sometimes leads to creative solutions to business problems instead of a more narrow focus on the legal issues. With Altman Weil noting in its 2016 Transition Report that roughly 65% of large law firms are offering LPM training of some kind, firms must go beyond training and begin coordinating LPM and other types of improvement activities to distinguish themselves in the marketplace.

Creating knowledge that has competitive value

Once a Legal Project Management program is in place with standards and protocols, lawyers acquire the habit of working within a framework and off a playbook, which allows them to adopt subsequent improvements that provide more value to clients and wider margins for the firm. Engaging in scoping and planning activities often leads to the creation of templates and checklists, which can then be reused on subsequent projects for other clients. Formalizing the flow of activities in process maps can help organize these inputs into their appropriate phases and serve as a communication device to train new team members and address unexpected events. Furthermore, a focus on project management often kick starts the use of matter types, the coding of time entries to phase and task codes and the capture of other matter attributes which inform value stream maps and ultimately refine pricing arrangements.

As more lawyers begin practicing project management, what will distinguish law firms in the future is the process knowledge gained through dialogue in areas such as the triple constraint, communication, and the application of lessons learned. Since dialogue takes time and requires teamwork both at a client team and practice level, law firm's will likely need ongoing executive engagement and support to reinforce its importance. By looking at each of these three areas, one can see how a more coordinated approach – one that combines matter management with process efficiency – can meet both the short term and long term needs of clients and create the edge firm's are seeking in the marketplace.

Triple constraint

One of project management's signature principles is the triple constraint, usually illustrated using a triangle that describes the interdependency between the scope, time, and cost of a project. Changing one of the legs of the triangle, either by increasing or decreasing its value, will cause a change in at least one, but sometimes both of the other constraints. In a law firm, the supervising attorney is responsible for documenting how a project's sponsor prioritizes these three areas and monitoring the project's scope, budget, and timeline. As a tactical approach to matter management, changes are communicated as early as possible in order to make the best decisions on how to proceed and to minimize surprises that could damage the overall relationship.

From a process design perspective though, the triple constraint ignores the underlying assumptions that cause this type of interdependency to occur. Since process improvement is focused on eliminating waste to increase both the velocity and quality in workflow, changing the design can in fact have a positive effect on all three at once. One of the keys to refining processes and central tenets of legal project management is making the implicit, explicit. By identifying specific resources and subject matter experts who can more cost-effectively perform certain tasks, and evaluating how a team's playbook can efficiently utilize these resources, business analysts and project managers working together in a coordinated manner can prevent or mitigate the impact of the triple constraint.

An example of this occurred during a pilot program in Husch Blackwell's mergers and acquisitions practice, where a team of lawyers applied the tools and techniques of Lean Six Sigma to uncover the drivers of cost and quality in the transaction. Initially, it seemed that many of the techniques applied during a typical closing scenario would be equally useful during planning. However, as the team mapped out the process according to a standard set of variables and identified areas of wasted and repeated effort, it became clear that simply managing the existing flow was not sufficient. Only by changing some fundamental aspects of the transaction's design by reducing revision through standard formatting, by mapping information collected from the client or other parties during interviews, and by staging language vetted by subject matter experts, were the team able to reduce the overall anticipated cost, timeframe, and frustration that often leads to deal fatigue. It is this kind of dialogue that is needed within project management programs to create the type of knowledge that has competitive value.

Clear consistent communication

In a law firm and law department setting, excellent communication is paramount when managing large tranches of work. By scoping matters, identifying stakeholder roles and responsibilities, and developing a communications plan, legal project management goes a long way towards providing clear and consistent information to the right people at the right time in the right format. Standardizing the type, frequency, and format of status updates in particular also places in-house counsel in a better position to discuss outcomes and provide updates to their superiors and business unit management.

However, if the standard process is quite manual, the sheer volume of matters, metadata, and status information may overwhelm lawyers on all sides. Granted, some law departments are fortunate enough to have enterprise matter management systems in place and can extend those systems to outside counsel. For those departments who haven't invested in that type of software, utilizing the expertise of business analysts and technologists to streamline the process can help alleviate the burden of manual reports without jeopardizing the delivery of consistent, reliable information. Even law departments who have enterprise software to facilitate communication and reporting sometimes need more custom solutions that go beyond their software's capabilities to achieve their business objectives.

At Husch Blackwell the legal project management team has had a number of opportunities to partner with clients by exchanging ideas, offering suggestions, and working side by side with business analysts and developers to build applications that standardize communication protocols and customize quarterly reporting. These efforts have streamlined matter intake, accelerated status reporting, enhanced the client's profitability in transactions, provided customized budget to actual analytics on the basis of a matter's attributes and reported on cost allocation within the client's business structure. In certain cases where Husch Blackwell coordinates the activities of other outside counsel firms, the broader team has assisted partners in designing solutions that even offload some of the administrative burden from the law department to the firm. Diving deeper into the process and technology can create additional efficiencies on top of those initiated by legal project management and reduce the overhead and frustration of handling large volumes of work.

Lessons learned

In a large law firm one of the most commonly discussed but least successfully applied techniques of project management is collecting and disseminating lessons learned during the closing phase of a matter's lifecycle. Ideally, these activities would include the updating of project plans, templates, checklists, and other tools to document both new tasks and assumptions and to identify resources useful on subsequent matters. Once these tasks are complete, the supervising lawyer would then invite the primary stakeholders to a post-project or retrospective session. During this meeting, the team would review the primary objectives and results and discuss their successes and mistakes and other exceptional circumstances. One of the team members would typically record the salient points and provide a summary of the team's recommendations, which could be searched through an intranet portal.

Anyone who has spent time in a large law firm will tell you that it can be very challenging to complete these tasks during closure and hold a meaningful retrospective session that contributes the type of knowledge that is valuable to other projects and the rest of the practice. Generally speaking, these sessions fail as knowledge management efforts because there is tremendous pressure to start working on other matters and few incentives to spend non-billable time after the completion of a matter. Other obstacles include a lack of objectivity, the reluctance of associates, paralegals, and support staff to speak freely, and a focus on execution versus the process itself.

Effective project management relies heavily on historical information and experience. Since information decays over time unless it is documented when the incident occurs, lessons learned should be captured throughout the lifecycle of the project, as root cause analysis is applied. Embedding knowledge management within each phase of a project's lifecycle also allows the supervising attorney to monitor its progress at stage-gate reviews and set aside time for dialogue in status meetings.

Then, during closure a final lesson's learned session would be more productive as lawyers discuss the knowledge captured throughout the project and consider how they could improve communication, collaboration, and other intellectual assets. Finally, setting the expectation that the matter's managing lawyer will meet with the client to listen to their feedback on the matter would create more accountability in conducting post-project review.

Reimagining service delivery models

Coordinating these other knowledge based activities requires understanding the inter-relationships between the links in the value chain and how those activities are shared among the law firm's business units. Intellectual assets increase in value as they are used and exponentially increase in value as lawyers tacit experience is transformed into explicit resources and then used to refine another's tacit knowledge. Thomson Reuters concurs; "Such a redesigned approach to legal services – combined with a pricing model based on outcomes (results) rather than inputs (recorded time) – could significantly improve both the competitiveness and profitability of those law firms willing to take these issues seriously." Once this dynamic of the spiral of knowledge takes hold, it becomes extremely difficult for competitors to emulate a firm's strategy or offer clients more attractive alternatives.

For legal project management to become a strategic asset, law firms must explicitly build in a greater emphasis on developing process knowledge than is typically found in many program offerings. Legal project management can provide clients the predictability, transparency, and efficiency they need, but only if there are standards in place and there is a higher level of coordination across the functional areas of the firm. Tom Baldwin, a partner with Fireman & Company observes; "With five plus years of often-failed attempts to address the problems in isolated ways, we are entering the next phase where integrated actions will finally yield the results that have largely escaped firms. By integrating efforts around pricing, LPM, and practice technologies, firms can maximize the return on their investments in these areas and create a sustained level of service delivery improvement not found in most current efforts that are conducted in isolation." Firm's investing in a more coordinated approach should formally recognize process knowledge as one of the LPM program objectives and create incentives to capture and share knowledge while working on matters under the program.

References

1. Citi Private Bank and Hildebrandt Consulting LLC, "2017 Client Advisory: How Firms Will Succeed in 2017 and Beyond", December 13, 2016. See: http://amlawdaily.typepad.com/2017CitiReport.pdf.
2. Georgetown Law Center and Thomson Reuters, "2017 Report on the State of the Legal Market", January 12, 2017. See: http://legalexecutiveinstitute.com/wp-content/uploads/2017/01/2017-Report-on-the-State-of-the-Legal-Market.pdf.
3. Altman Weil, "2016 Law Firms in Transition", May 18, 2016. See: http://www.altmanweil.com/dir_docs/resource/95e9df8e-9551-49da-9e25-2cd868319447_document.pdf.

Chapter 7: How KM staff can help drive successful legal project management initiatives

By Antony Smith, founder of Legal Project Management Limited

The emergence of the discipline of legal project management (LPM) is relatively recent. I have heard it said that in terms of its overall maturity, LPM is now where KM was about 10 years ago. Frankly I am in no position to judge whether this is actually true but what I do know is that there are far fewer dedicated legal project managers in law firms compared to KM staff, and the adoption of software support tools for LPM is far lower than it is for KM.

Experienced KM staff should be in a good position to help with any LPM initiative in a law firm and they are often tasked in doing so. They understand what it takes for best practices to spread. They can also help directly with supplying best practice case plans, templates for all kinds of documents, and generally complimenting and enhancing the core skill-set of fee earners.

The aim of many LPM initiatives is that, ideally, fee earners apply project-based methods almost without thinking, simply as part of following the firm's standard way of working. As with any project, an LPM initiative needs to be planned, managed, and executed well if a firm is to reap maximum benefit from it. This can be something of a catch-22 for some firms as they do not have sufficient project management skills available to help improve the legal project management skills of their lawyers.

Knowledge management is itself quite a wide discipline and KM practitioners will often have diverse backgrounds. Some KM staff will feel very comfortable leading LPM implementation or improvement projects, and others will not. It is inconceivable, however, that a law firm will not seek to involve KM staff in some way when trying to develop its LPM capability.

So what factors should KM staff bear in mind when striving to make a success of an LPM initiative? Before I try to answer this question, I would like to remind you briefly what LPM is and why it is becoming increasingly important to law firms. I will then set out a project-based approach and provide some practical tips which should help make any LPM implementation project a successful one.

What is legal project management?

Legal project management by definition is the application of project management principles, methods, and techniques to the delivery of legal services. It can help lawyers better manage their individual matters and their practice as a whole.

This definition is deliberately broad. In operational terms LPM can cover a multitude of things, ranging from legal workflow process improvements to developing fee earner skill-sets (such as estimating and scoping matters).

Why do law firms want to develop their LPM capability?

The benefits of applying LPM are widely known. However, given that it is still relatively early in the overall development of LPM, realizing these benefits consistently remains challenging for law firms. Nevertheless, it is clear that LPM helps law firms to:

- Increase the predictability of fees, leading to increased confidence when devising pricing strategies;
- Estimate costs more accurately;
- Control costs more effectively;
- Identify and manage risks better;
- Become more agile when responding to client needs;
- Develop more streamlined legal delivery processes;
- Communicate more effectively with clients;
- Enjoy more productive relationships with clients;
- Improve realization rates;
- Increase profitability;
- Protect, and increase, business with current clients; and
- Acquire new clients.

In order to capture these benefits, law firms need to:

- Train fee earners and other related professionals about LPM principles and techniques;
- Create frameworks, processes, and procedures which support a project based approach to legal service delivery;
- Continue to develop the LPM *skills* (which is not the same as knowledge) of all relevant staff; and
- Embrace IT support systems (especially workflow and data analytics) whilst appreciating that successful implementation of LPM does not depend solely on IT.

How to start improving LPM capability

If your firm is about to begin an LPM initiative, either introducing LPM into the firm for the first time or seeking to improve existing LPM practices, what factors are likely to improve the likelihood of successful outcomes?

Think in terms of "projects"

Leaving aside servicing "business-as-usual", at any one time there will be numerous projects going on in most law firms. Sometimes these projects are not even recognized as such. They may be referred to as "IT upgrades", "business improvement initiatives", or simply as "another round of marketing".

The fact is that any commercial endeavor can be classified, and therefore managed, as "a project". Blithely "doing stuff" which ties up resources without putting some project control around it is a recipe for disaster. So, the first thing to do is to recognize that tasks and activities which together make up an "LPM initiative" is "a project" in its own right. Hence someone needs to be in charge of the project and have accountability for deliverables.

Recognize that project management alone is not enough

Unfortunately, collecting and ordering tasks together as "a project" and putting some management control around it cannot guarantee successful outcomes. Even when organizations are enlightened enough to create "projects" and apply some form of project management to them, projects can often fail to deliver their hoped-for benefits.

What makes this situation rather depressing for professional project managers is that the main causes of project failure are well known, as are the key things to do to avoid such failure. There have been a number of studies which have investigated project failure and listed the most common reasons why projects fail. The list provided by the UK's (former) Office of Government Commerce (OGC) has been cited widely.[1] This list was first published in 2002, and it is still relevant today. According to the OGC at the time, projects fail because of:

1. A lack of clear links between the project and the organization's key strategic priorities, including agreed measures of success;
2. A lack of clear senior management [and Ministerial] ownership and leadership;
3. A lack of effective engagement with stakeholders;
4. A lack of skills and a proven approach to project management and risk management;
5. Too little attention to breaking development and implementation into manageable steps;
6. An evaluation of proposals driven by initial price rather than long-term value for money (especially securing delivery of business benefits);
7. A lack of understanding of, and contact with, the supply industry at senior levels in the organization; and
8. A lack of effective project team integration between clients, the supplier team, and the supply chain.

While this list comes with the caveat as being "aimed at those managing or otherwise involved in the delivery of projects across Government", it looks a pretty comprehensive list to me and, I'd argue, one that is also relevant to commercial organizations of all kinds, including law firms.

Aligning LPM with law firm strategy

I cannot imagine a law firm with a strategy which does not place clients, and the best means of servicing them, at its core. Legal project management is all about improving legal service delivery. Therefore, aligning any LPM initiative with a firm's strategy should be relatively straightforward.

Securing support of senior business owners and managers

In theory it should be equally straightforward to secure the support of senior business owners and managers. After all, an LPM initiative will (almost certainly) be aligned to the firm's strategy and all senior management staff buy into this, right?

Of course, and this is by no means confined to law firms, this is not always the case. In fact it often falls upon the project team to secure full and enthusiastic support of senior stakeholders – something which some KM teams may be all too familiar with! Who might these senior stakeholders be and how can a project team make sure they are properly engaged with the project?

Project sponsor

In project management jargon, a project sponsor is the internal champion of a project. So, in a law firm, for any kind of LPM initiative it is almost certain that a senior partner will be the project's sponsor. The most important aspect of a project sponsor's role is to engage with other senior people within the firm (most obviously their fellow partners) and ensure that the project is fully resourced throughout. In effect, the project sponsor is the project champion.

Now if the project sponsor is genuinely committed to LPM and has volunteered, perhaps even pushed for, the role of sponsor, then obviously the main issue for the project team is to retain their backing rather than securing it in the first place.

If the project sponsor has been asked to sponsor the LPM initiative by other partners they may be fairly lukewarm about LPM. This can be an awkward, but not impossible, situation. Perhaps the best advice here is to keep reminding the project sponsor of the benefits that LPM can bring to the firm and their practice area. Indeed, it may be best to focus on their practice area when considering any potential LPM pilot project. If you can ensure the project sponsor can see some early benefits from LPM then they are much more likely to become fully engaged in the project and a more vocal advocate of LPM in the firm.

Other senior managers

LPM initiatives will often cut across departmental boundaries. People with roles in fee earning, business development, operational support (including IT and Finance), and of course KM, all have a legitimate interest in LPM initiatives. As a result, managing, or being part of, an "LPM initiative team" can be quite challenging. So how can this challenge be met and overcome?

I would suggest, and this will probably come as little surprise to experienced KM professionals, that particular emphasis should be placed on effective communications with team members, right from the start. Communications which are regular, clear, and concise not only advance the project, but also help promote a culture of transparency and collaboration amongst the team.

Communication effectiveness (or lack thereof) can make or break projects. It is estimated that professional project managers spend between 70 and 90 per cent of their time on communications. Indeed, communication effectiveness is the key differentiator between the very best project managers and the rest.

Break projects down

A standard approach is to break projects down into a number of stages. It is quite common to see five distinct stages referred to: Initiation, Planning, Execution, Delivery, and Close. A project manager is responsible for steering a project through each of these stages.

From a project manager's perspective, most effort is (or should be) expended during the first two stages. It is during these stages that the scope of the project is defined, resources gathered, and a timetable agreed with the project sponsor and other key stakeholders (i.e. those who are affected by, or have a material interest in, the project).

Project initiation

The aim of the project initiation stage should be the agreement and signing-off, of a project initiation document (PID). This document captures the essential features of a project with reference to items such as project aim, scope, approach (i.e. how the work is to be performed), resources, budget, key risks, proposed schedule, and outline communications plan. Most importantly, a PID will state the acceptance criteria for project completion.

Project planning

During the planning stage more detail is added to the outline plan and timetable encapsulated in the PID. Perhaps the best advice which can be given here is to go through the PID and ask repeatedly "what if" (for example: What if you do not get access to all resources? What if the timeline begins to slip?) and plan alternative scenarios based on your answers.

I would also suggest you talk, and walk plans through, with trusted colleagues. They may be able to spot things you have missed and perhaps offer reassurance that you really have asked enough "what-ifs"!

Project execution

During the project execution phase project managers will be monitoring and controlling project progress. They will, if they have sufficient authority to do so, make changes to the project to keep it moving forward. They will also communicate this progress to all stakeholders regularly and escalate issues which are beyond their authority to the project sponsor.

During the execution stage a project manager needs to keep on top of all project issues and monitor risks (logs are set up for these). Another vital aspect of a project manager's role is managing scope creep. A project which changes during its lifetime is not necessarily a bad thing; indeed, it is to be expected. However, any changes in scope need to be agreed clearly with the project sponsor and other key stakeholders.

Project delivery

If the planning has been thorough enough and execution diligent, project delivery should be relatively straightforward.

Projects will usually be made up of several delivery stages and indeed different types of deliverables. For example, LPM initiatives are likely to involve some legal process re-design and fee earner training (both areas in which KM teams are likely to be involved on some level), and IT support.

Project close

Project close is made up of several elements: the project sponsor signing off acceptance, the project team reviewing the project, and archiving useful project artefacts for potential re-use on other projects.

Some tactical ideas for LPM implementation

The above is a skeletal outline of a formal project management approach, but what tactical steps can KM teams take to help improve the chances of a successful LPM implementation project? The following is a list of suggestions:

- Start small with some pilot projects; pilot with teams based in discrete practice areas and, ideally, pilot with those who are most interested in LPM (such people do exist – you just need to identify them in your firm);
- Encourage those who have experienced the benefits of LPM in pilot projects to spread the word to other areas of the practice;

- When designing LPM frameworks and practices it will probably help to think in terms of high level workflow. For any given practice area consider:
  - What activities are required to complete the most common matter types;
  - Who will (or who should) perform these activities; and
  - What outputs are expected from these activities.

Consider what kind of software support would help your LPM initiative. There are a number of software vendors which offer LPM support solutions. Alternatively you may wish to:

- Investigate the feasibility of creating a software support tools in-house;
- Give serious consideration to branding your LPM initiative such that it becomes a recognizable aspect of the firm's practice; this helps make people in the firm feel as though this version of LPM is theirs (which it is) and they will identify with it more readily; and
- Be prepared to engage outside experts who can offer LPM training, coaching, implementation, and consultancy advice. While it is essential that your firm "owns" its LPM implementation, objective advice from outside the firm can be invaluable.

A version of this article first appeared in Roche, H. (e.d.), Legal Knowledge Management: Insights and Practice, *ARK Group, 2013.*

References

1. See: www.dfpni.gov.uk/content_-_successful_ delivery-newpage-50.

Chapter 8: Project management plus process improvement – The multiplier effect

By Catherine Alman MacDonagh, JD, CEO and founder of the Legal Lean Sigma Institute LLC, and creator of Legal Lean Sigma® and The Legal WorkOut™

Others in this book make the case for project management and explain why, where, how, and when to implement it. This chapter focuses on the multiplier effect of combining project management with process improvement. In fact, to a PI practitioner, even project management is a process! As such, the design and implementation of a project management program is a process improvement project too.

Any book on project management in the legal profession or elsewhere should address something right away: it's all well and good to have excellent project management skills, but without an optimized (or even good) process, all the great project management in the world can only deliver limited success. Of course, there is little point to having a good (or even excellent) process if there is no one to manage it well. PI and PM should be employed together.

One might well argue that all lawyers already use project management and employ processes (also known as "best practices"). Of course they are – how else would work get done and service delivered? However, we believe that every process will benefit from improvement – and that includes the way each organization structures an overall program and develops then employs good project management skills. More often than ever now, we help build sustainable programs that not only combine continuous improvement, practice management, pricing, and innovation, but rely specifically on the methodologies and tools of PI and PM to structure programs that are uniquely designed for each client. We often begin by building on the current tools and language and aligning with strategy and client requirements.

Consider this scenario: You are a client who's hired two partners in the same practice areas in a firm. Both get their work completed on time.

However, they each have developed their own approach, best practice, forms, and/or way of working, etc. One might do the work profitably with great service and a well-coordinated, high performing team. The other might burn out associates and paralegals and have no idea as to how much effort it really takes to do and deliver the work. How does this affect the client experience? What are the consequences of this variation? What about from the firm's perspective?

The PI/PM connection

Lean Sigma and project management, which are separate but complementary disciplines, should be used together to ensure greater alignment between the law firm/legal department and client through better, structured, and far more frequent communication.

Process improvement helps us determine the best way to carry out a certain kind of work to achieve efficiency, excellent quality of work and service, high probability of successful outcomes, and predictability. As soon as we start to describe and measure a process, we will begin to see things that could be improved, either in the client's eyes or the firm's/department's eyes or both. In fact, most of our processes fall far short of their potential and improving them will benefit *both* the client and the firm/department.

Project management is, essentially, a role and set of skills which ensures that the lawyer, firm or department, for each matter, selects and uses its best processes appropriately, and then actively manage the client relationship, schedules, staff, and deliverables throughout the matter. Everyone would agree that it is a waste of valuable experience to start each matter as if it had never been done before. Thus, we should start with a standard process and then modify it to suit each matter and to deliver what the client(s) require(s).

Process improvement

A process is a describable, repeatable sequence of activities that generates an outcome. Our processes are the way we create and deliver value to the client and are the embodiment of our knowledge as to the best way we know how to do something.

Process improvement is the systematic practice of first analyzing a process to understand how it is *currently* carried out, then searching for issues, problems, and opportunities in the process and prioritizing them. Once prioritized, tools and techniques are employed to solve priority problems or to capture significant opportunities. Finally, the new process must be controlled so that it delivers the anticipated benefits. To a process improvement practitioner, nearly everything qualifies as a process, from the mundane routines of everyday life (like making coffee or tea) to incredibly complex processes involving multiple operations, people, organizations, and so forth (such as class action law suits).

In the words of W. Edwards Deming, who was known as the Father of the Quality Revolution, and was responsible for the first application of statistical quality control principles to a non-manufacturing environment, "If you can't describe what you are doing as a process, you don't know what you are doing." It's easy to extend this thinking to include project management – if you can't describe what you're doing as a process, you certainly can't say you're managing either the process or the projects that use it.

What Lean Sigma practitioners often find is that the processes people think are in place are not or, more accurately, that they are not functioning the way we thought they were. Most of the time, we find that each person has his or her own process and that the processes take much longer, costs more, and/or doesn't meet client requirements to the degree and in the manner we expected.

As Henry Ford famously said, "Most people spend more time and energy going around problems than in trying to solve them." What we see in the way the legal profession works is that most people spend more time and energy solving problems created by processes than improving them. This is often considered part of "legal project management," but to a Lean Sigma practitioner, it is a sign of a process that is either broken or at least not performing well.

In many cases, we have seen that what started out to be a decent practice has changed over the years. Usually, this is due to workers that compensate with well-intentioned (and sometimes heroic) workarounds due to the failure of the process to support the person working with it.

While Lean Six Sigma for the legal profession is worthy of its own book (see *Lean Sigma for Law Firms*), it is useful to define it here. In short, Lean is about creating simpler, faster processes and reducing (if not eliminating) waste. Six Sigma is focused on controlling and reducing (if not eliminating) undesirable variation. With Lean, we simplify processes, reduce the number of steps, maximize process speed, and greatly improve productivity – we focus on doing the right things and eliminating waste in processes. In this way, we ensure that we maximize resource efficiency.

The two disciplines are about doing the right things (Lean) and then doing those things right (Six Sigma). Put together, Lean Sigma is about deciding the best way to do something and then always doing those things correctly.

Note that we do not gratuitously reduce or standardize anything; not every step or part of every process should be standardized or controlled as tightly as another step in the same process – this demonstrates that the application of PI and PM is both art and science. There may be plenty of steps that require us to allow for a lot of latitude as we need to build in room for variation based on the lawyer's experience and knowledge. Other steps require little to no judgment and are therefore good candidates for tightly controlling variation. Every case or matter does not need to be approached anew: it isn't efficient and it also contradicts in actions what we say to our clients, prospects, and referral sources in terms of our great experience.

Lean Sigma uses a disciplined problem solving approach known as DMAIC. This is an acronym for the five steps of Define, Measure, Analyze, Improve, and Control – which are always performed in that exact sequence, without ever skipping steps. It is practically a mantra for process improvement practitioners and provides the framework for a process improvement project – all of which must be managed well by a Team Lead with good project management skills.

- **Define** the problem and why it needs to be solved – here is where we carefully work through all the elements of a project charter.
- **Measure** the current performance of the process – we measure the process in two dimensions: the performance level, or how well the process meets client expectations (process performance), and the resource requirements, or the time, people, equipment, etc., to carry out the process (process efficiency).
- **Analyze** the opportunities to reduce waste or variation, identifying root causes.
- **Improve** the process by developing solutions and identifying, implementing, and validating process changes.
- **Control** the process by implementing methods to ensure improvements will be sustainable and that the improvements are translated into benefits.

When delivering a process improvement project, we move though DMAIC's proscribed sequence of steps, each of which includes helpful ways of thinking through and analyzing many business questions and situations. Throughout the project, we must manage the project logistics, schedules, and deliverables, plus the team and all the various people and roles associated with it.

What should be clear about the DMAIC methodology is that it provides the structure for managing a process improvement project. It even includes change management and communication through the effective use of checkpoints known as Gate Reviews. These safeguards include the all-important meetings with a Steering Committee, which take place at specific points during and the conclusion of each phase. This ensures that we are communicating as we progress with our projects and that we are employing good change management techniques.

A process improvement project team meets with the project sponsor and a Steering Committee that is typically comprised of cross-functional leaders in the firm to pass through "gate reviews" or "toll gates." In those meetings, the Steering Committee holds the team responsible for completing specific deliverables that are required in each phase and ensures the team has addressed all important considerations.

As such, rather than complete a project from start to finish and then deliver the results, the approach demanded by process improvement is for the team to regularly check-in with their project Sponsor and engage in gate reviews with a group of decision makers that stays with the project from start to finish. This format builds in regular and ongoing communication for the duration of the project and provides a forum for the team to share their work as it progresses from diagnosing, measuring, and analyzing the process to finally developing improvement ideas. The stakeholders also have opportunities to contribute their perspective, expertise, and resources on an ongoing basis – it is built in to the process of process improvement and the project management of a process improvement project.

In fact, we employ good project management skills from the outset of a process improvement project, making sure that the project scope and expectations are clear, that there is strong sponsorship and ownership, and that the problem (and the impact of the solution) can be measured and quantified.

Project management for both legal and process improvement work

When we develop the capacity to do process improvement work, we can employ project management skills to select the best processes, tools, and skills to be able to carry out our ideal process every time. Essentially, project management gives us the steps (or process, if you will) and tools to review and select the right processes and then apply them appropriately to each matter. Then, project management involves actively managing schedules, staff, and deliverables to deliver high quality work on time and under budget to achieve specific goals.

Timothy B. Corcoran, principal of the Corcoran Consulting Group and faculty and affiliated consultant of the Legal Lean Sigma Institute, defines project management as "the process and activity of planning, organizing, motivating, and controlling resources, procedures and protocols". As such, the way we do project management may be considered a process that should be in a state of continuous improvement for any learning organization.

Corcoran explains the six steps of project management as follows:

1. Define objective (what constitutes a win for the client – and also the legal team?);
2. Define scope and constraints, e.g. budget, timeline;
3. Establish the project plan. (Identify standard, variable, and volatile tasks; establish task timelines and budgets. What is on the "critical path"? What resources are necessary, including a project manager?);
4. Execute the plan (track efforts, time, budget, results);
5. Continuously monitor performance, change management (including regular communication and establishing a continuous "feedback loop"); and
6. Review and improve. (Learning organizations focus on improvement over time.)

Case studies: The multiplier effect of employing PI/PM together

When we combine Lean Sigma with project management, we develop the ability to do the right things, the first time, every time. The combination is used to develop more than just best practices – in fact, process improvement and project management can lead to innovation and significant competitive advantage.

Some lawyers may initially resist the notion that their work can be reduced to a series of steps where predictability of activity and budgets are possible. It is important to recognize that their concerns have some merit, however, they are fairly quick to recognize how many legal processes have standardized components such as completing forms or obtaining follow-up information that, when streamlined, can improve the work product produced and the service delivered to the client. In addition, the rising number of PI/PM successes are too significant to ignore. So the issue is no longer whether PI/PM should be employed; it's when and how.

No law firm, legal department or other organization approaches the building of a PI/PM program the same way. There are many excellent examples of organizations of all sizes and practices of all types that have achieved successes as the result of employing them together.

One of the best examples of a service that realized extraordinary benefits from combining process and improvement and project management is from commercial real estate attorney Rebekah Fisher. Fisher, currently of Fisher Matthews PLLC, formerly of Waller Lansden Dortch and Davis, Dinsmore & Shohl LLP, developed an excellent process to prepare, negotiate, and execute a great number of commercial leases each year for a large retailer client. She improved her process of handling commercial real estate and then managed it in a way that resulted in the highest levels of client satisfaction and excellent profitability for her practice and firm.

To perform this work profitably using a fixed fee structure for the portfolio of this work, Fisher focused on improving and standardizing her process, communications, forms, and leases. She explained that she uses only very organized and efficient timekeepers, which involves staffing with the lowest-cost resources capable of doing each activity for each engagement. Detailed data about the effort it takes to both do and deliver this work is kept, which allowed Fisher to continually refine her model process and very effectively manage the work and resources.

The results are impressive. Fisher reports that they improved their response time from the receipt of the client's request to producing a draft of lease to either the same or the next day. They also reduced the overall time it takes from their receipt of the client's request to the execution of a lease from 168 days to 62 days.

It is important to translate improvements into benefits: Fisher's fast, reliable results have allowed the client to open stores an average of 8 weeks earlier. This is worth tens of millions of dollars in increased revenue for their client. In short, in addition to the fact that Fisher's process allows the law firm to deliver this service profitably and reliably for a low fixed fee, their client's high satisfaction with the results has them singing her praises. This, in turn, resulted in new, referred business.

An improved OFCCP audit process was one of the many projects tackled at Ogletree, Deakins, Nash, Smoak & Stewart, P.C. This project was championed by practice group leader Leigh Nason, whose practice includes representing federal contractors and sub-contractors in compliance evaluations and administrative enforcement actions triggered by the United States Department of Labor's Office of Federal Contract Compliance Programs (OFCCP).

After measuring and analyzing many aspects of the process, the team drew inspiration from great coaches and sports teams to develop creative improvements and solutions. Examples included developing a "playbook" with a current roster/directory, and specific "plays" (checklists, forms, etc.) so that quality assurance and consistency is guaranteed regardless of the client or attorney working on the project. The team also clarified guidelines regarding credits, opening matters, and rates and ensured that the premium rates for this niche practice work were not "watered down" by insurance rates.

"An effective communication strategy and specific procedures for working with referrers that included checkpoints, exchanging client development information and otherwise ensuring that we continue to keep referrers "in the loop" regarding clients entrusted to us were developed and implemented. Additionally, standardized communications were established for consistency in messaging within the practice area and the firm. This includes simple but critical items such as file naming conventions across the practice area team and organizing data files in a highly-specified file structure on a shared drive with standardized file names and email subjects. The new process also ensures that relevant information is stored on the firm's document management system and managed on a dedicated drive for practice group matters," says Nason.

The team also developed new practice group codes to better identify various components of practice area in order to measure profit, utilization, growth trends, and contractions. Another outcome of the project was established standard operating procedure of formalizing the relationship with the client on new matters, e.g. use of specific language (on documents such as engagement letters) to clarify details and logistics.

Peter Hitson, director of legal process innovation at Wilson Elser Moskowitz Edelman & Dicker LLP, explains that the firm's legal process innovation work is seen as a natural evolution of their focus on customers and their need for both effective and efficient legal services. Founded in 1978, Wilson Elser grew to nearly 800 lawyers in 26 offices across the United States, one in London and European affiliates.

Hitson says that "Wilson Elser includes Legal Project Management (LPM) and Legal Process Improvement (LPI) as part of its long-term vision and formal strategy. We have a rich base of existing processes, strong technology and practice groups aligned around key practice areas that help to share capabilities beyond our regional offices. What we wanted was greater uniformity in applying LPM and LPI as a core competency."

In her article, "5 Firms Take Bold Approaches", Susan Saltonstall Duncan reported, as part of a series of four related articles that appeared in the *ABA Law Practice Magazine* (Volume 38 Number 6 – November/December 2012), on firms that made a decision to do things different from the very start.

In her interview with Pat Lamb of Valorem Law Group, which is widely regarded as a firm that has led the "new normal" movement, Duncan reported "In 2008, when Patrick Lamb and three partners thought about starting a new kind of law firm focused on clients and value, they knew that a critical framework would be in pricing their services in a radically different way than their predecessor BigLaw firms (and most law firms) did. When they started setting fixed prices for their trial and litigation services, they realized that they needed to focus on the cost of providing those services – or they would never be profitable. Things would now have to be done faster, more efficiently and better than before."

One of the cornerstones of Valorem's business model is that project management and process improvement are essential. Duncan further reports, "From the outset, lawyers took typical cases and produced process maps to delineate each step in the process. For example, before lawyers start to do any discovery on a case, they talk to the client first to establish an approach that is consistent with the client's desired outcome. The focus is on a full case assessment first, which dictates the fee, but more importantly, the value proposition and the winning strategy. The Valorem Toolbox provides tools for trial, budgeting, fee estimating and decision trees."

Conclusion

Many in the legal profession ask: "in which discipline should we invest and engage first, process improvement or project management?" The simple answer is that there is no one, right way to begin, but why not learn and employ both simultaneously? This is precisely why the Legal Lean Sigma Institute developed the first and only certification courses that cover Lean, Six Sigma, and Project Management together.

If we must choose one or the other, I usually recommend engaging in process improvement first. This way, an organization begins to improve processes and simultaneously develop project management skills while delivering the project. After that, the firm or department can train project managers and others using optimized processes.

Whether your organization begins with process improvement or project management, eventually, both must be employed for the firm/department to fully realize the benefits of either one. We attain a multiplier effect when we combine process improvement and project management: we have better, more standard processes that are well controlled and appropriately applied to every engagement. This enables us to achieve a high level of performance and both do and deliver our work in ways that deliver value for all concerned.

Reprinted with permission. Some content appears in Lean Six Sigma for Law Firms *by Catherine Alman MacDonagh.*

Chapter 9:
Overcoming IT mutiny – Obtaining fee-earner buy-in for a new project management system

By Helen Bunker, divisional director of private law at Blake Morgan

Key points

1. Shop around and consider longevity of the supplier before buying
2. Pick a system which can accommodate different fee-earner preferences
3. Run a series of presentations and encourage everyone to provide input
4. Put in time to customize the product and deliver real value

Mergers often trigger the need for a review of IT systems and this was the case when Piper Smith & Basham merged with Hughes Watton and then Boyd Hutchison in 2004 to form Piper Smith Watton.

The motive for the mergers was to grow and strengthen our expertise by adding breadth to our niche property, corporate, and litigation practices. However, the disjointed systems we had inherited needed replacing and we required the systems and business processes in place to support an integrated operation. This became the prime driver to our search for a new accounting and case management system, which began in 2005.

Over the past few years, I recognized that the best way to maximize the return on IT investment is for people to embrace these technologies as fully as possible. In terms of software, the more flexible it is to accommodate different working practices and fee-earner preferences, the more likely you are to achieve your goals.

In the immediate post-merger era of 2005, when we sought to replace the old systems, we took advice from a consultant to define our requirements, checked the Law Society's software solutions guide and evaluated different suppliers. We eventually settled on two best-of-breed systems for practice and case management.

There was an immoveable deadline in 2006 for the start of the financial year to get the new accounting system in place. We therefore prioritized the accounts side over case management and the conversion of data from the old systems' databases became the priority.

Part of the rationale for selecting Solicitors Own Software's (SOS) Practice Manager was that, although not the cheapest practice management system, I believed it would be flexible enough to grow with us. I was impressed at the development potential of the system and the enthusiasm of the provider. The thinking was that there would be a better return on investment than with some of the cheaper products available on the market at the time.

At the time of going live in 2006, the case management system was not as far advanced as we would have liked. I was head of the private client department and took the lead in implementing the system. However, the software was less well suited to other areas of the firm. Several fee-earners, including my former senior partner, were skeptical of case management and resolute in choosing to only use the software for time recording and accounting.

Meanwhile a period of consolidation of software suppliers began and our case management provider was acquired by a larger corporation. Support unfortunately deteriorated, as did our satisfaction. By this time, SOS' plans to develop a document and case management system – Connect – were underway.

A new system

In 2009, we took the decision to replace the case management system with SOS Connect, which would integrate fully with the existing accounts system. The 2009 project was a lot smoother. This time we could dictate the go-live date, fitting the project around the competing demands of running a business.

By this stage, document and case management systems had become far more mainstream and were viewed with less suspicion. We ran a series of presentations to the firm about the new system so that everyone could understand and air any concerns plus address issues prior to going live and provide input for further development. This time we achieved real buy-in from fee-earners.

Features such as key performance indicators and the way relationships are set up in the system impressed us. I felt the modern look and feel of the software, together with its integration with Microsoft Outlook, would make the system more appealing and an easy win, which turned out to be the case.

A driver in deciding to move to the new system was the huge growth in the use of email by solicitors between 2006 and 2009. For example, within the corporate and commercial property teams, around 90 per cent of incoming mail is now electronic.

The reliable audit trail that we now have for emails – where incoming and outgoing messages are automatically tied to a matter – quickly won people over, while providing the opportunity to improve efficiency and risk management.

While we don't automatically time record for incoming emails, we do have a routine for outgoing mail. Through Outlook, the new system reminds fee-earners to record time, although it is not the default setting. The reminder helps to reduce the amount of email thinking and preparation time that is often lost or leaked, allowing fee-earners to accurately record time spent.

Softly, softly

The changeover to the new system was made in July 2009. The reception was very different to the previous case management system, with the whole firm more involved. Standard processes for file opening, time recording, documents, account postings, and billing have been adopted by everyone.

Only two departments – corporate and retail property – are not wholly utilising the case management system, as the work is more bespoke and fee-earners prefer to file only their final documents into the system.

I've learnt that having a flexible system is crucial to match the varying needs and different paces of change across departments. Finding an approach to systems implementation that matches our culture has been key to maximising the system's acceptance.

The private client department has become a showcase because of our extensive use of the system. People can see what we are achieving and the adaptability of the software. For example, around two thirds of the correspondence is based around standard letters within the system, which can accommodate our requirements fully. Letters can be bespoke rather than having to conform to a one-size-fits-all system template, while offering the benefits of not having to create them from scratch. By getting to know the software well, sharing that knowledge and demonstrating successful application in my department, the goal is to encourage others to get the most from the system too.

Our former senior partner, who had been skeptical in 2006, has used the new system since day one and become a product champion, which has helped engender the widespread support for the system that we have today.

As yet we have not quantified the return on this particular software investment. IT is critical to our business and the markets we serve and we have always strived to keep ahead, given the size of the practice, and have several IT projects running concurrently.

For example, we moved to digital dictation in 2003 and today can dictate remotely via our Blackberries. Fee-earners also use them to provide clients with the instant communication and service levels they have come to expect and now demand. We have been outsourcing dictation since 2004 to provide fee-earners with 24-hour support as an extension to our in-house secretarial services, again investing time and effort in refining the system to deliver real value. We are also rolling out speech recognition software which can also be accessed on lawyers' Blackberries.

Measuring impact

While it is difficult to quantify the impact of any one project, it is clear to everyone that we have achieved the fully integrated firmwide system that we sought and have the capability to continuously refine processes. We have also achieved a single point for support.

Fee-earners are able to access far more information for themselves, in theory improving productivity. Where fee-earners are working in teams, they all have access to "the file" and are able to see and respond to the same information. It is now far easier to retrieve information after a matter is closed (as opposed to requesting a hard copy file from an off-site storage facility).

Our firm was awarded Lexcel accreditation in 2002 and has successfully maintained it since then. Given the Solicitors Regulation Authority's ever-increasing compliance requirements, the new system is assisting dramatically with compliance and risk management, complementing our established procedures.

The system has further streamlined the processes online, such as for high risk undertakings and file reviews. It also enables us to capture a far greater level of detail than before. For example, the copious amount of time-sensitive information required by professional indemnity insurers (for property matters in particular) is now centralized and readily available.

Continuous development

We are currently integrating automatic filing for Blackberry emails into the system, which is in direct response to the growth in remote working.

Another project is to bridge the gap between credit control and fee earners. Credit control is now run through the system so that fee-earners are easily able to see any actions taken by the credit control department, such as an email chaser, letter, or statement. Equally, any comments or reminders made to clients by the fee-earner can be noted and shared.

This means that a credit controller can instantly see that a fee-earner has talked to the client about an outstanding balance, or noted details of a payment promise. In the past, fee-earners and credit controllers worked using their own systems, meaning time could be wasted and information lost between the two teams.

We now have a system where key performance indicators can be reviewed in real time. We have created and maintained an open culture and team ethos. Heads of departments and partners have access to departmental and firmwide information from their desktops and can readily identify any blips and trends.

We also present a performance versus target graphic to fee-earners as they log off, as a reminder to ensure time is recorded accurately and to see if they are falling behind or ahead of targets.

The recession has resulted in clients expecting a better and faster service – and to pay less for it. So we have to find a better and more efficient way of operating. We are able to delegate more to secretaries and paralegals, while managing risk with everything logged in the system.

A key benefit is that it is flexible, which has enabled us to take a softly, softly approach, matching the varying requirements of departments and fee-earners, whilst ensuring we retain a bespoke approach, tailoring matters to the clients' needs.

It is very gratifying to see use of the system expanding and information flowing freely in real time, helping our business to run more efficiently. And we've only just begun.

Achieving fee-earner buy-in for a new system

- **Don't be overambitious with go-live dates** – remember any implementation has to fit in with the competing demands of running the firm. Don't be afraid to push back the date if the project isn't ready.
- **Ensure your project team includes constituents from all areas of the business.** You may think you know how different practice areas work, but that is not always the case. At the beginning of the implementation process, get as many people involved in demos as possible so that they can understand the features, impact, and

opportunities which the new system brings to the business. We encouraged an open culture and team ethos, as well as transparency and visibility of information. Enabling people to express any concerns and provide input for future developments at an early stage of the project is also a good idea.

- **Choose a flexible system** to match the varying needs of different departments and be willing to accommodate different paces of change throughout the firm. Getting everyone involved and thinking about how the software could be adapted to their exact requirements helps to ensure the software is widely used and a return on investment is made. It's important to find an approach to implementation that matches the culture of your organization.
- **Focus on an obviously beneficial feature** – in our case, the integration with Microsoft Outlook and unified systems for the whole firm – to enthuse people and build aspirations. Looking for quick wins enables you to build on success. Early in the process, we were able to roll out standard procedures and processes such as for file opening and time recording, documents, accounts postings and billing.
- **Create a showcase of one area of the business** so others can see how much can be achieved. Sharing knowledge from the showcase and demonstrating success was an important factor in encouraging others to get the most from the system. Identifying a respected product champion from an unexpected source to win over those less enthusiastic about adopting change proved beneficial too.
- **Don't think the project ends at go-live** – that's when it really takes off and new ideas start to flow. Be ready to react to this and implement changes to ensure continued growth and development. Put a system in place for continuous improvement and welcome ideas from all sources.

A version of this case study first appeared in Managing Partner *magazine in November 2010. Fully revised and updated in 2017.*

Chapter 10:

Lean and agile – How legal project management can transform client services

By Karen Dalton, senior enterprise project manager, and John Duggan, senior legal project manager at Seyfarth Shaw

Key takeaway points

1. **Address lawyer resistance to project management.** Convincing some lawyers to embrace change by using any sort of project management approach can be daunting. Many lawyers feel that thorough planning slows them down and may not be efficient due to the many unknowns in legal. In reality, that is exactly why they need project managers who use the "agile" framework.
2. **Be selective when hiring legal project managers.** One of the biggest challenges can be finding people with the right skill set to perform the role of legal project manager. They need to have a legal background, strong project management skills, and some exposure to "agile". You cannot judge by résumés alone when interviewing candidates – you will need to consider some intangible qualities.
3. **Get comfortable with "agile".** The agile development model may have its roots in software development, but it has proven valuable in many industries, including legal. One of the core tenants of the agile framework is flexibility. Success requires a willingness to live in the grey and getting comfortable with being uncomfortable. If a particular approach or tool is not working, don't be afraid to change course until you achieve your goal.
4. **Choose tools carefully.** Lawyers may roll their eyes at some project management tools such as Gantt or PERT charts. Fortunately, there are a host of low-cost tools that lawyers will find more complimentary to the way they work.

Imagine working in an industry where opposing forces are trying to derail you each step of the way on most of the projects you are managing. Welcome to the world of legal project management.

Our legal project management office (LPMO) has been faced with the seemingly insurmountable challenge of managing an ever-growing portfolio of legal projects, where formal and traditional project management approaches didn't quite fit the adversity we encountered from external parties (such as opposing counsel and government regulators). It became obvious very quickly that flexibility and agility were going to be critical.

Picture this: 76 projects, five experienced project managers and constantly-changing requirements and expectations, with new projects being proposed every day and no end in sight. Traditional project management techniques would bury even the best of project management offices (PMOs).

Our firm's commitment to the principles and practices of lean six sigma (a process and data-driven approach to performance improvement) led to the creation of our own client service model, branded Seyfarth*Lean*. The programme combines the core principles of lean six sigma with robust technology, knowledge management, process management techniques, alternative fee structures, and practical tools.

Project management principles and expertise have played an important role in the overall success of the Seyfarth*Lean* programme. The firm's journey to become a leader in the legal project management (LPM) arena has been a circuitous one that has led us through a variety of approaches and disciplines.

Creating the LPMO

The firm's venture into project management began by setting up a small PMO, with the simple goal of improving the overall success of several large-scale internal-facing projects. The natural place to start was with project managers skilled in the principles and practices of project management, based on the de facto industry standard: the PMI's Project Management Body of Knowledge (PMBOK®) (hereafter referred to as traditional project management).

Shortly after the introduction of the PMO, Seyfarth embarked on its lean six sigma journey. Our entire PMO was invited to join the inaugural class of six sigma green belts (the initial certification). During this initiative, the value and importance of project management and project managers became readily apparent.

Our project managers integrated the disciplines of project and process management. Voice of the client, process mapping, data analysis, metrics, root cause analysis, $y=f(x)$, and kaizen became a part of our daily lexicon.

With our green belt certification and a couple of proven successes in partnering with attorneys and their clients, our PMO slowly transitioned from inward facing to outward/client facing. Not only did we transition in function and focus, but we also transitioned from being the PMO to being the LPMO.

As we did so, we began to realize that some of the traditional project management disciplines – while valuable in some instances – were contributing to our growing pains. The rigours of traditional project management, with its detailed documentation, waterfall-based phases, change control, and paperwork, were interfering with delivery in the fast-paced and often unpredictable world of legal service delivery.

Lean implies simplicity and efficiency, and our LPMO needed to become more efficient if we were going to be able to keep up with the demand for our services being fuelled by the Seyfarth*Lean* initiative.

Success begets success and competency attracts work. Soon our project managers were spending close to 80 percent of their time on client-facing projects and more of our time became billable to clients. We spent countless hours on process mapping and setting up client extranets, matter dashboards, and project task lists.

Gone were the multi-page project charters, detailed project plans laying out in detail a project in its entirety from beginning to end and robust status reports. In their place were simple one-page forms and web-based tracking tools.

Three-day planning meetings were replaced with one-hour kick-off meetings. Status reports changed from detailed "stop light" rollup reports to emails with bullet lists, which were designed for easy consumption by our internal and external clients using mobile devices.

Our LPMO barely resembled the PMO of the past. We had entered somewhat uncharted territory. There were no models for us to follow, no industry best practices to draw from, but what we were doing was working and we knew that we were headed in the right direction.

Our team discovered and utilized various tools and techniques that would allow us to be flexible in our approach to satisfy varying client expectations, while still demonstrating good project management protocols and concepts. As we looked around the world of project management, we discovered, quite by accident, agile project management.

Agile project management

Agile project management is based upon a set of simple principles (see box: Principles of agile legal project management). Although agile was conceived with software development in mind, its principles and concepts have been applied in numerous industries outside of software development. There is no one set of agile methods – in fact, there are dozens of new methodologies that have adopted the agile principles.

As the name implies, agile management is flexible. The agile principles are akin to the theory of "less is more". Agile is characterized by short iterations, regular feedback cycles, less emphasis on documentation, early and continuous delivery of value, and self-organising and self-managing teams. These characteristics, while difficult for some legal professionals to accept, are precisely why they can be so effective in the delivery of legal services.

One of the primary tenants of agile is that we can't possibly know everything at the beginning of a project and hence trying to build an end-to-end plan is often futile. Rather than developing detailed project plans broken into discrete phases (also known as waterfall planning), agile promotes the identification of near-term deliverables and getting started just as soon as you know enough to begin. The project team then reviews any backlog and commits to delivering as much as is possible within the next time iteration. Each iteration focuses on the delivery of a potentially fully-functional work product.

If there is one word that aptly described our LPMO, it is agile. We did not set out to adopt agile project management, nor did we try to retrofit our PMO to utilize agile. In a manner of speaking, we were accidentally agile.

Seyfarth*Lean* principles of agile legal project management

- Delight clients through early and continuous delivery of valuable solutions that meet or exceed their needs and/or solve their problems;
- The best solutions and improvements emerge from carefully examining the "voice of the client";
- Welcome changing or evolving needs throughout the project. Agile processes harness change for the client's competitive advantage;
- Aim to deliver solutions and/or improvements frequently, from daily incremental improvements to weekly or monthly, with a preference to the shorter timescale;
- Business people, legal resources, and the client must work together throughout the project;
- Deliver projects through motivated individuals – give them the environment, tools and support they need, and trust them to get the job done;

- Client engagement and feedback is the primary measure of progress;
- Continuous attention to excellence and client satisfaction enhances agility; and
- Regularly reflect on how to become more effective (through the use of lessons learned), then tune and adjust behaviour accordingly.

Note: With acknowledgements to the Principles of Agile Software Development

Challenges faced

Our journey and evolution into becoming a lean and agile law firm was not without its challenges. These included:

1. Building a model without precedence;
2. Lawyers' inherently change-resistant nature; and
3. Finding and grooming qualified project managers.

1. Lack of precedence

We likened our department's efforts to a start-up company: the biggest challenge being that there was no existing model for our Seyfarth*Lean* agile legal project management approach.

One of the core tenants of our LPMO philosophy and of the agile framework is flexibility. We found success through our willingness to live in the grey area and being comfortable with being uncomfortable. If a particular approach or tool was not working, we were not afraid to change course until we achieved our goal.

Depending upon a project's complexity, the project management sophistication of our internal and external clients as well as our formal "voice of client" interviews, we select the appropriate solutions from our Seyfarth*Lean* LPMO toolbox: the right resources, processes, and tools. We then use a "sense and respond" approach to managing the project, often swapping out tools and approaches as needed to add value and ensure success.

One might think that approach resembles chaos and disorganization. However, the essence of agile is to embrace and respond to change. We do not just conduct one voice of client session, but are constantly soliciting feedback from the client. This encapsulates the sense and respond approach which has been a cornerstone of our success.

2. Lawyers' nature

In our efforts to make matters more efficient under our Seyfarth*Lean* programme, we were reminded that lawyers are trained to:

- Challenge everything; and
- Base decisions on precedence.

Convincing some lawyers to embrace change by using any sort of project management approach can be daunting. Many feel that thorough planning slows them down and may not be efficient because of the many unknowns in legal.

In reality, that is exactly why they need project managers who use the agile framework. We know that they can only plan so far ahead, that matters do not follow a defined path and that new evidence can change a game plan in a moment's notice. But we plan for those variables in alignment with client-defined value and guidance.

One of the keys to successfully navigating this challenge is to introduce agile project management slowly. Start simple. Meet with your stakeholders and create a checklist of tasks and assignments. Continuously solicit feedback from your stakeholders and do not be afraid to change what is not working. The lawyers will appreciate that you are allowing them to focus on the area where they possess the highest value – the actual practice of law, while you take care of task management. You will achieve buy-in by demonstrating success.

3. Appointing project managers

Another one of our biggest challenges has been finding the people with the right skill set to perform the role of legal project manager. It is difficult to find people who have a legal background, strong project management skills, and some exposure to agile.

We learned that we could not judge by résumés alone when interviewing candidates. We needed to consider some intangible qualities. Our sense and respond philosophy is so essential to our success that we have to make sure our new hires meet the following criteria:

- **Have a high level of emotional intelligence.** Are they self-aware? Can they process verbal and non-verbal cues appropriately? Do they appear to have good intuition? How will they handle constructive criticism and suggestions for change?

- **Are flexible in their approach to projects.** How well do they respond to fluid situations? If they have only practiced the traditional waterfall project management methodology, for example, we would have to consider whether they would have the ability to adapt to our environment.
- **Possess a mature sense of confidence and the ability to influence** a team of high-performing individuals to achieve success. Could we see them sitting alongside attorneys or across the table from our clients?

It is difficult to evaluate all of these qualities in an interview. The most important quality is flexibility and the ability to make good judgement calls in an ever-changing project environment. If you have a sharp person who is willing to listen and try new methods, you have won half the battle.

Impact on the firm

Our use of the Seyfarth*Lean* agile framework has resulted in positive outcomes for the firm. We have found that:

- The ramp-up time for projects is shorter, as we do not have the need to understand every bit of minutia before stepping in to assist;
- Communications are more effective and efficient – we document the items that are essential to the project's success and do not get bogged down in templates, forms, and procedures;
- With our streamlined approach, our staff are able to manage several projects at once, as opposed to being mired in the smallest of details on only one or two projects;
- Clients and lawyers are delighted with our right-sized approach, knowing that we are always focused on the efficient delivery of legal services – we are deft at avoiding the bulk; and
- There is an increase in the quality of our work product – by focusing on value-added tasks and continuous improvement, we are able to produce better results for our clients.

Lessons learned

1. Know your audience

While lawyers generally know their clients well, they are often surprised at how much their clients know about lean six sigma, project management, and even agile. Clients expect exceptional legal expertise, but what they are most interested in is how the firm is going to do their work.

Clients are very interested and receptive to innovative value-added services that deliver results. Project management, when done well, can be a key differentiator.

2. Relationships are critical to success

Lawyers can be very protective of their relationships with clients and consequently can be very reluctant to introduce project managers to their clients. In addition, lawyers are taught to challenge everything: proof is required. We had to win them over with innovative ideas, hard work, and client-valued results.

Introducing agile, while innovative, can be seen as radical. Initially, it may be best to keep agile legal project management behind the scenes and concentrate on the value delivery it facilitates. Eventually, building relationships through agile with both the firm's lawyers and clients can lead to dramatic results.

3. Flexibility and adaptability drive success

While it is generally common practice to develop an overall strategy in a legal matter, detailed project plans are often not effective with legal projects. While you are planning for success, opposing parties are planning for their success (which generally does not align with yours). Sometimes you never know what is going to happen next.

Agile embraces change and provides the mechanisms for early and regular delivery of value, no matter how the scope may change.

4. Adapt to the way your lawyers work

Lawyers like to get started right away with doing the lawyering. Traditional project management is perceived as slowing them down.

Agile frameworks like scrum (iterative and incremental frameworks for managing projects) support lawyers' mindset. As soon as you have enough information and knowledge about what is needed next, you can get started. Agile's short iterations with regular feedback cycles fit right in with the lawyering mindset.

5. Look for tools that work

Traditional project management tools (like Microsoft Project) can be unnecessarily complicated and cumbersome for many legal projects.

There are several easy to use, low-cost alternatives that lawyers seem to favour (despite their similarities to MS Project).

Some of the tools that we have found particularly useful are SmartSheet, One Pager Pro, Sharepoint, TaskMap, Quickbase, and Mindview. Each serves a different purpose and may not be necessary on all legal projects. We continue to look for and evaluate new tools every day.

A version of this case study first appeared in Managing Partner *magazine in March 2013. Fully revised and updated in 2017.*